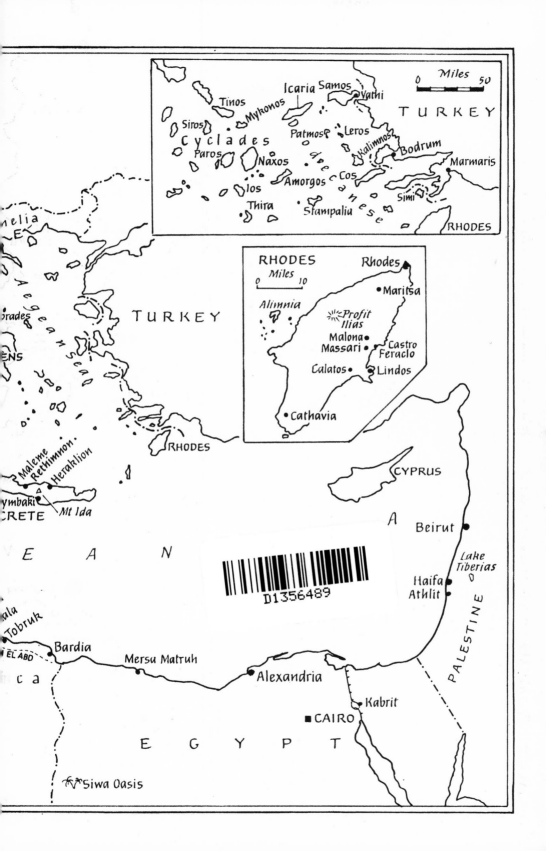

HE WHO DARES

HE WHO DARES

RECOLLECTIONS OF SERVICE IN THE SAS, SBS and MI5

by

DAVID SUTHERLAND

with a Foreword by

LORD JELLICOE

LEO COOPER

First published in Great Britain in 1998 by
LEO COOPER
an imprint of
Pen & Sword Books Ltd
47 Church Street
Barnsley
South Yorkshire
S70 2AS

© David Sutherland

ISBN 0 85052 643 4

Typeset by SetSystems Ltd, Saffron Walden, Essex
Printed in England by Redwood Books, Trowbridge, Wiltshire

Dedication

This book is dedicated to Commander Michael St John, DSC, and to the Officers, Petty Officers and Seamen of His Majesty's Submarine *Traveller*, who plucked Marine Duggan and me from the sea off the Island of Rhodes on 17 September, 1942. Commander Michael St John survived the war. Sadly, HM Submarine *Traveller* and her crew were lost on a later war patrol in the Mediterranean.

Contents

It is night. It is flat calm. Two men silently enter the water and swim towards a submarine. Both are starving, exhausted, emaciated. They have had no food or water for three days. They feel the onset of fever. They are the two survivors of a raiding group of twelve which has destroyed fifteen Italian aircraft which have been attacking shipping and bombing military targets in Egypt. Somehow, they have evaded capture by the 30,000-strong enemy garrison.

After 45 minutes swimming the submarine spots them. The stronger of the two men swims rapidly to the afterplane. The weaker man grabs a line thrown to him. Both are hustled quickly by the crew along the casing and below. Immediately the sub crashdives. There are two depth charge attacks.

Shaken but undamaged, the sub heads for Beirut.

The place is the island of Rhodes – the date 17 September, 1942, when Rommel's well-seasoned army is at El Alamein, 60 miles from Alexandria, with its eye on Cairo.

One swimmer is a Black Watch Lieutenant, the other a Royal Marine. Both are 21.

Foreword

by
LORD JELLICOE

I count it a rather special privilege to have been invited by my wartime comrade-in-arms and very old friend, David Sutherland, to contribute a brief Foreword to his fascinating recollections of a full, varied and exciting life of no mean achievement.

I did not know the young David, not having had the privilege of an Eton or a proper Sandhurst education. Likewise, post-war, our professional paths did not cross. However, it was always a pleasure to meet this friend whom I admired so greatly and to talk about our wartime years together in the Special Forces. And I was, of course, well aware of the important role which he had played as Colonel in command of 21 SAS, one of the Territorial SAS Regiments to which David Stirling, the Founder of the SAS, rightly attached so much importance.

Again, I did not meet David in the first year of the war, although I have read with admiration and pleasure his understated account of the role he played as a nineteen-year-old Black Watch Platoon Commander in the Retreat to Dunkirk. It makes good reading.

However, from the autumn of 1940 until the end of the war I saw a great deal of David. We were together in No. 8 Commando. We travelled out together to the Middle East with the great David Stirling, who, since he seldom left his cabin, we christened 'The Great Sloth'. And when our Commando was disbanded I kept abreast of his subsequent and daring activities – his participation in the abortive raid on Rommel's Headquarters and his exploits in Tobruk. Thus when we met early one June morning in 1942 in German-occupied Crete, David was someone I knew pretty well and about whom I knew a good deal. In his book he states, 'One always remembers most clearly the first encounter with Crete.' True. But I shall also always remember that Cretan encounter with him.

Soon after that David played an outstanding role in the successful, albeit costly, SBS attack on enemy airfields in Rhodes, an episode brilliantly, albeit modestly, recounted in his book.

Given that background, it was a very real pleasure for me to know that David was to be one of my three Squadron Commanders, when, on April Fool's Day, 1943, following David Stirling's capture, the small SBS was re-formed under my command and became the enlarged Special Boat Squadron.

David tells superbly well and with great accuracy (I wish I had his memory!) the raiding role which his 'S' Squadron and indeed the Special Boat Squadron itself (later to become the Special Boat Service Regiment) played in 1943 and 1944, be it in Crete, be it in the Aegean, be it on the Mainland of Greece or be it in the Adriatic, and the contribution that those continuous raids, together with the activities of the Long Range Desert Group and the Greek Sacred Squadron, made towards containing German forces in South-East Europe when they were needed elsewhere.

I shall not elaborate on his account. It speaks, and speaks well, for itself. And it is shot through with the generosity of its author. This is apparent in the tributes which he pays to those who helped us – to the Navy, be it the more regular naval forces, British or Greek, or be it the remarkable Levant Schooner Flotilla. It shines through in his gratitude to all the

Greeks who supported us in those days, often at grave risk to themselves. As he writes: 'They guided us, they fed us, they sheltered us and they died for us. No one in the SBS will ever forget this.' And of course this generosity of spirit, this feeling for those under his command, is clear from all he writes, not least of his thoughts as he returned from his successful 'S' Squadron mission in the Aegean in early 1944 when he said to himself, 'These officers and men are special. One can take them on SAS operations anywhere in the world and they will perform well. I am incredibly lucky to be leading them.'

Yes. David Sutherland was incredibly lucky to have those chaps, both officers and, very much, men, under his command. I was lucky, too, to have under my command many remarkable men – Ian Patterson, John Verney, Walter Milner Barry and the heroic Dane, Anders Lassen, to name but a few. I was also quite particularly fortunate to have had David as one of my leading Squadron Commanders – a born commander, supremely professional, calm in a crisis, utterly courageous and one who had a very special feeling for everyone under his command. Thus, when I was required to nominate my successor to command that unique unit, the Special Boat Service Regiment, I have never in a fairly long life been faced with an easier decision. Clearly David Sutherland was the right man for the job. And so he proved, as he has proved in his many subsequent assignments which he recounts so well.

JELLICOE

Preface and Acknowledgements

My tall, extrovert, teenage grandson James approaches. In his hand is a well-worn copy of *The Filibusters* by John Lodwick. By common consent this is the best account published so far about the wartime activities of the Special Boat Service. James has read it from cover to cover. I know I am about to be quizzed closely on its contents and my part in the SBS story. Originally, SBS was a small enemy-held beach reconnaissance and inshore sabotage unit, using canoes. In December, 1942, SBS in the Mediterranean was taken over by David Stirling and became part of the SAS.

With a wry smile, James asks, 'Why were the SBS Adriatic operations so disappointing?' I explain the political and military difficulties and frustration when highly geared, trained and motivated Special Forces are injected into a raging Civil War between Royalists and Communists in Yugoslavia and Albania, and cannot take sides. A Balkan nightmare, repeated in Bosnia.

This book is for my grandson James and his generation. They are interested, I am pleased to say, in the wartime history and tradition of the Special Air Service Regiment and its operational development since.

After the war I had 25 interesting years in the Security Service, MI5. Also, I commanded 21 SAS Regiment (Artists Rifles) TA from 1956–60. I was able to change the role of

SAS in the Reserve Army to behind-enemy-lines reconnaissance and reporting. It is now time to include something about this.

The idea of writing this book has substantial support from my sister Susan Collins, family and friends. A whole raft of amusing SAS Regimental Association characters and colleagues with whom I have close wartime operational links agree.

At the start I must thank particularly the distinguished Commander of HM Submarine *Traveller*, Michael St John, and his crew. By his skill in placing his submarine in enemy-infested waters, and waiting a long time for the redoubtable Marine Duggan and me to swim out, we made a quick getaway from Rhodes. If we had failed to reach *Traveller*, the Italian depth-charges would have killed us. Next morning our mangled bodies would have been found floating in the sea, amid much Italian jubilation.

The other person who has given me a lot of valuable original material about Operation ANGLO is George Vroohos, the well-known lawyer and historian living on Rhodes, a bright and delightful man whom I first met when visiting Rhodes in 1986 to look over the ANGLO deadly open ground. He has become an expert on Operation ANGLO and its local impact. He sent me two interesting documents: Italian Governor General, Admiral Inigo Campioni's report to Rome on ANGLO – Sheila Gruson has kindly translated this – and Vroohos's own detailed report on ANGLO which the attractive Greek ladies C. Variadis and B. Niotis have translated into English. Both are included in the book complete.

Some years ago the distinguished military historian, Barrie Pitt, who had served in 21 SAS Regiment, got in touch with me. He wanted to write a book about the SBS in the Mediterranean during the last war. He felt that *The Filibusters* did not provide the strategic background into which SBS operations fitted. We had long talks at 51 Victoria Road about the early 1942, 1943 and 1944 SBS operations in Rhodes, Crete and the Aegean. He asked for and I lent him three volumes of Operational Reports, personal accounts and photographs.

His book, *Special Boat Squadron – The Story of the SBS in the Mediterranean*, was published in 1983 by Century Publishing, London. It contains a lot of the original material I gave him. I am grateful to him for writing this book. I have used some of the details in his book in mine.

I would also like to thank Drs Carritt, Zilkha, McKeown and Thompson for keeping a watchful, jovial eye on my health, and Tanky Smith and Jason Mavrikis of the Special Air Service Regimental Association for keeping me straight on dates, places and people.

Above all, my sincere thanks to Mary Young for transforming my totally baffling handwriting into a fine manuscript.

Glossary

A/C	Aircraft
A/T	Anti-tank
BLO	British Liaison Officer
BMMG	British Military Mission to Greece
DCLI	Duke of Cornwall's Light Infantry
DLAW	Directorate of Land/Air Warfare
GRF	Greek Raiding Force
HDML	Harbour Defence Motor Launch
JRRU	Joint Reserve Reconnaisance Unit
KKE	Greek Communist Party
LFA	Land Forces Adriatic
LRDG	Long Range Desert Group
LSF	Levant Schooner Flotilla
MG	Machine gun
MTB	Motor torpedo boat
OP	Observation Post
RFHQ	Raiding Force Headquarters
RHN	Royal Hellenic Navy
RTU	Returned to Unit
SAS	Special Air Service
SBS	Special Boat Service
SLO	Security Liaison Officer
SOE	Special Operations Executive
SOP	Standard Operating Procedure
TSMG	Thompson sub-machine gun
VCDS	Vice Chief of the Defence Staff
VCIGS	Vice Chief of the Imperial General Staff

1

Origins

1920–38

I am a lucky Scorpio and an unconventional, adventure-seeking Scot. My roots lie in two very different places – the rich farms and tidal estuaries of East Suffolk and the remote and heather-clothed upland hills and pastures of Peeblesshire in the Borders.

My links with Suffolk lie via the Quilters – a bright, influential land-owning family then living in great style at Bawdsey Manor, a hideous, Victorian clifftop mansion overlooking the wet and windy 'German Ocean'. Norah Quilter, with a Plantagenet nose, was my grandmother. In 1898 she married the taciturn William Miller, scion of a prosperous family of Victorian textile manufacturers based in Preston, Lancashire. The Millers had several properties and houses in the hills overlooking Morecambe Bay and in one of these, Singleton, Norah and William lived. They had two children, Ruby, my mother, and Eustace. Sadly, before long William died. Norah, now a young and lonely widow and loathing the Lancashire downpours and gloomy-looking countryside, soon decided to return to her family, the Quilters, and the benign Suffolk climate. For some years she rented houses near Ipswich.

In 1910 Norah married Guy Vivian, a round-faced Major in the Grenadier Guards. Together they bought a small country estate and an attractive, white-painted Georgian house with several cedar trees nearby – Foxboro' Hall, near Woodbridge – deep in 'Quilter territory'! As it happened, Guy and my father, Arthur Sutherland, knew one another. They had served together in India as ADCs to the Governor of Bengal.

During the 1914–1918 war many country houses in England became nursing homes, caring for officers and men wounded in action. Foxboro' was one of these.

In August, 1914, when the war began, Arthur Sutherland, a Lieutenant in the Black Watch, was living in Cape Town as an ADC to the Governor. In those days all aspiring young officers wanted to be ADCs. The work was interesting, not especially onerous, fun and good for one's career prospects. Uneasy at being stuck far away from the fighting in France, Arthur felt strongly that he should be on active service with his Regiment, particularly as there were battle casualties. He got to France in January, 1915. On 9 May, 1915, there was a major British attack to take Aubers Ridge, vital high ground strongly defended by the Germans. The attack failed and in the process there were many casualties. Arthur Sutherland was hit by a machine-gun bullet in the right ankle. There were so many wounded from that battle that it took three days for the ambulance trains to reach hospital. By that time gangrene had set in. If he had not been astonishingly tough he would have died on the train, as many others did. As it happened, he lost his right leg above the knee. He was 24.

About this time Guy Vivian had been wounded and was recovering at Foxboro'. Hearing that his friend Arthur Sutherland had been badly wounded himself, Guy got in touch with him and suggested he come to Foxboro' to recuperate there. This he did.

Working as a young nurse at Foxboro' was Norah Vivian's daughter Ruby. She was very pretty, Arthur Sutherland dark and handsome. He had just been awarded the Military Cross for his bravery in the Aubers Ridge attack. She was there to care for him, help him get about and dress his ugly wound.

Thus their romance began. Being remarkably fit and most determined to get back into the war, Arthur made a rapid recovery and, having quickly mastered the intricacies of an artificial leg, rapidly got himself into a staff job in France. Intelligent, experienced and highly efficient, he became in 1917 Assistant Military Secretary to FM Lord Haig at GHQ France, for which, in due course, he received the Order of the British Empire and the Légion d'Honneur. During this time he was writing to Ruby at Foxboro'. In 1919 they got married. There were some family misgivings over this, particularly from Norah Vivian, on grounds of the 9-year age gap. She was right. Ruby was a parochial child of 19 just out of the schoolroom, Arthur a high-powered, sophisticated 27. I was born in October, 1920.

The Sutherlands came from Thurso in Caithness. My grandfather, George Sutherland, was educated at Westminster where he did well as an athlete. He wanted to go on to Cambridge but had to interrupt his studies in order to join the family firm in Calcutta, which at that time was losing money. As a young bachelor he shared digs with Rudyard Kipling.

Bright and hard-working, my grandfather was one of the group of distinguished Scottish civic and commercial leaders in the early years of the century in India. He was one of the mercantile members of the Viceroy's Council in Lord Curzon's day. He was Sheriff of Calcutta, for which he was knighted, and head of the firm Begg Roberts & Co, trading in tea and jute and handling various profitable agencies. Not a military man by nature, he happened to marry, in turn, the daughters of two prominent army officers who later became Generals, John Glynn from Wimborne, Dorset, in the Rifle Brigade and James Wolfe Murray from Eddleston near Peebles, in the Royal Artillery. Nellie Glynn was my grandmother. Sadly she died of a puerperal fever after giving birth to my father in Calcutta in 1891.

In 1919 my grandfather retired from India, moved his

business affairs to London and rented a house in Mayfair. He had no property in Scotland, so he rented Cringletie near Peebles which was his second wife Elizabeth Wolfe Murray's family home. This is an imposing 1875 Victorian fudge-coloured wynstone mansion by the Edinburgh architect Bryce, with tiled turrets in the French château style. Cringletie is set on a gentle hillside above Eddleston Water. With the house came a stunning view of a jumble of hills ten miles to the south beyond Peebles, some interesting-looking cottages, many acres of field and woods, immaculate lawns and a fine fruit and vegetable garden. As Elizabeth had good taste she set about decorating Cringletie and making the house more comfortable, and warmer. The Regular Sutherland tartan is a dull, uninteresting dark blue and green. Using old vegetable dyes, Elizabeth had some dress tartan woven in Peebles with a more striking light blue and vivid green. Some of this was made into jackets, skirts, trews and kilts for the family and for covering cushions. The Sutherland crest is a cat 'Sejeand Guardian' and the motto 'Sans peur'.

I was happy and contented, but for some reason, not a robust child. However, I survived penumonia at 2 and peritonitis at 4. My father would have liked to have remained in the army but had to retire in 1922 because of his disability. He then joined my grandfather in Begg Roberts and Co., in which he made a successful business career. We were then living in Harlow, Essex, so he could go easily to the city and back each day by train. This family harmony was shattered out of the blue when I overheard my parents having a furious row. Tiptoeing downstairs into the sitting-room, I came upon my mother ashen-faced, in tears, clutching a small dog, my father towering over her shouting, face contorted with fury and his well-known short-fused temper letting rip. Bewildered and frightened, I ran upstairs to my room to be joined there by my mother, who tried to explain what was going on. 'Don't worry,' she said, 'your father is tired and not feeling well.' This was the first indication I had had that my parents' marriage was fast collapsing. I felt this new, unwanted situation was incomprehensible and sad. It was 1927 – I was 7. An acrimonious divorce followed, giving my mother custody of me, with time to be spent with my father. My mother and I moved to a gloomy and cold house near Colchester, while I waited to go to preparatory school. Being an only child I had no one in the family to talk to about my problems. But my mother and, particularly, my wise grandmother Norah understood well the reason for my depression and occasional lapses into silence. They designed for me an exciting and interesting programme of activity within the warm family embrace of Foxboro' and the many interesting people who lived and worked on the estate. For that I am eternally grateful.

At the age of eight I went to Rose Hill School, Banstead, Surrey. There were about seventy-five boarders. I recall the trauma of getting into the school train and leaving my tearful, cloche-hatted mother behind on the Victoria Station platform. However, I soon began to assimilate into the new, different and in some ways welcome scene. I was among boys of my own age whose regular company I had hitherto missed. Set in its own small farmland, the school was run on traditional three-terms-a-year lines, with work and games equally important. One recalls the cold, unwelcoming dormitories, hard hospital beds, a thin blanket, white enamel washing basin and matching jug, dark brown lino on the floor. A plump, uniformed matron handed out spoons of 'Virol' for me to put on weight. In those days my fair hair had a pinkish tinge about it. Wearing the pink school cap with 'RHS' in letters on the front, my appearance was, to say the least, bizarre. There were few boys at the school with divorced parents. This meant that on 'parents' visiting day', one Saturday each term, they came on different days, my mother on Saturday and my father on Sunday. To me this arrangement was at first sad and later ridiculous. One longed for a huge lunch in a local hotel or, in the summer, a fantastic hamper picnic under the trees with both parents there, as was the norm at the school. But this was not to be.

I always had generous support and consideration from both my parents, nevertheless, and went steadily up the school, becoming for some reason good and successful at soccer. The school was run by a memorable contrasting duo, Hughes and Buckley. Thomas Hughes, short, with a small black Hitler-like moustache and built like a tank, was the prime mover. He was by nature aggressive, bright and a no-compromiser. Richard Buckley, on the other hand, tall, with a willowy figure and an impossibly vague manner, resembled the poet Shelley. They were known by the boys as the Führer and the poet! Lessons with the Führer, who taught Maths and French, were a terrifying experience – time with the poet, who taught Latin and History, far more relaxed and benefi-cial. Later I discovered that the poet had been at Eton with my father. And the principal and exceedingly difficult task for the poet at this time was to help me get into Eton myself, which, against all the odds, he did! I went to Eton at thirteen. By that time my father had married Joan McKechnie, an attractive, sophisticated lady by whom he had two children.

At Eton it matters a great deal who one's housemaster is. Either one is in a house in the mainstream of day-to-day school competitive activity, or one is in a house on the edge of things. I was lucky to be in the former group. Arthur Huson, a wise, port-drinking, cricket-loving bachelor of the old school, was one of the most experienced and successful housemasters of his day.

At the appointed hour at the start of my first half (term), I was taken by my apprehensive mother to take tea with Miss Holland, the House Dame (Matron). She wore a comforting-looking brown tweed skirt and matching cardigan – a plump, reassuring figure for terrified new boys to turn to for help, which she was. I noticed Miss Holland poured tea from an extraordinary-looking pot, a black china cat standing upright with clasped paws through which the tea was poured. At the time I wondered if this hideous-looking object would have any lucky significance for my fortunes at Eton! Perhaps it did.

For a raw newcomer the sheer size of Eton is daunting. Finding one's way to the right place at the correct time also was a problem at first. My amiable cousin Kenneth had come to Eton from Ludgrove School the half before me. He too was at Huson's and I remember him showing me the way to Lower Chapel where we prayed each day, and to various key classrooms and to Rowlands, where we sat down together at a small well-scrubbed table and devoured delicious bacon, eggs and sausages, followed by strawberries and cream – a 'strawberry mess' for which each of us paid threepence. My allowance was sixpence a day rising to eighteen pence when I was sixteen. The custodian of everyone's allowances at Rowlands was the intelligent manager, Jack. He knew to a penny the state of everyone's account. 'No, Mr Sutherland, you've overspent, you can't have anything till next week'!

One was quickly enveloped by the daily school routine. Boys' maid wakes me with a jug of warm water at 7. Struggling into Eton collar and jacket. Run/walk quickly to Early School at 7.30. Back to the house, Wotton House, an ugly, Edwardian monster overlooking the main football field, for an adequate breakfast at 8.15.

One quickly settled into the routine of daily life of work and games and quietly progressed up the school. There was plenty of inter-house sporting rivalry and banter, particularly between Huson's and Marsden's. There was the hilarious encounter when the rolypoly Huson passed the acerbic-looking Marsden in Common Lane going to Early School one magical May morning – 'Spring in the air, Marsden' – 'Spring in the air yourself!'

Unlike today, life at Eton then was easy and unhurried. There was no pressure and plenty of time to complete one's work, and enjoy cricket, football, squash and fives and make countless friends, many of whose company I enjoy to this day. One recalls Eton blanketed in winter fogs, spring flood marks on High Street walls, the smell of toast from the coal fire in one's room, the thrill of winning an important fives match with my cousin Kenneth, who had a marvellous eye, a picnic under Upper Club trees.

Believe it or not, as a boy I was scared stiff of water. This stemmed from two foolhardy happenings. One cold November day when I was seven I was cheerfully running along the Woodbridge harbour wall when I tripped over a rope and fell 10 feet into the icy water below. Luckily a strong RAF sergeant from Martlesham air base heard my mother's frantic screams and pulled me out with a boathook. I recall being carried soaking wet on my rescuer's shoulders up Woodbridge Hill to our house in the High Street, given a slug of brandy and put to bed. The second happened some years later when I was foolishly playing around in the River Deben at Kyson Point, when the tide turned and I began to float downstream. Fortunately my uncle's alert gardener saw what was happening and grabbed me to safety. Curiously there was, and perhaps still is, a cup awarded annually to the Eton house in which all the boys can swim. It was called the Nant cup! I remember sitting quietly in my room when the door was flung open and in strode a handsome, patrician figure wearing a white bow tie, braided tail coat and claret waistcoat. It was the head of the House, Michael Astor. I stood up to receive the well-deserved and anticipated rocket. 'Look here Sutherland – it's high time you learnt to swim. We failed to win the Nant Cup last year because of you. That *can't* happen again!' I look back on this absurd conversation with amusement, but it did get one going.

George, a splendid, patient, weatherbeaten-faced Waterman with a gold watch-chain and a straw boater with an Eton blue ribbon, gave me swimming lessons in Cuckoo Weir. I remember George telling me confidently one warm summer evening, 'You'll pass next time, Sir.' He was right. I did and we won the Nant Cup! As it happened, this was all just as well because a few years later in the Mediterranean on more than one occasion I had to swim for my life.

In the 1920s and 30s farms depended completely on the horse. There were no tractors. Fields were about 25 acres in size, bounded by ancient hedges thick enough to keep out cattle and sheep. There was no wire anywhere. The most important person on the farm was the horseman. At Foxboro' Ernie Nunn was horseman. This marvellous, powerfully built man had a nose like a Viking and a lined brown face. He wore corduroy trousers, hobnailed boots, tweed cap and a farmworker's smock. Sitting beside a plough run I remember the special hiss of the sharp blade as it cut through the light soil, and Ernie's grunt of satisfaction as he turned the huge Suffolk Punch round for a return run. There was a large industry supporting the horse, particularly smithies within walking distance, where elaborate wrought-iron gates were made for Foxboro' garden.

In the 1920s and 30s there was little inflation, a large British Empire in place and a strong currency, sometimes 5 US$ to the pound. For people with money living was surprisingly cheap. In such a situation an army of loyal servants and retainers, men and women with jobs secure for life, existed. These people were always around in my youth as part of the family. I remember mentally jousting at the whist table with the formidable Foxboro' housekeeper Ritches and taking a dram with the amiable John McKellar after a good grouse shoot. This satisfactory arrangement came to an abrupt end in 1945 with the election of a Labour government and the country's impoverishment due to the cost of winning the war.

My grandmother Norah ran an excellent house at Foxboro' in the Victorian tradition. She was bright, strict, well informed and popular. There was plenty of good food and she knew the importance to young people of an annual routine that never changes – Easter Sunday church service and chocolate eggs, summer fêtes, jumble sales and tennis with tea and cucumber sandwiches on the lawn, the house packed tight with people of all ages for Christmas with a huge candle-lit tree magically bedecked.

Often my great-uncle, the scholarly-looking composer Roger Quilter, was there, quietly tinkling 'O Mistress Mine' on the piano. He would say, 'David, join me singing,' which I did, off key! The house had its own special smell, burning applewood logs in spring, maturing Cox's apples in autumn, cedarwood smoke in winter. As Foxboro' was not intensively farmed, it was a paradise for birds' eggs, butterflies and moths. I collected these in the spring and summer and worked at my postage stamp collection in the winter.

On the way to church one passed an ivy-clad cottage. In it lived Charlie Hills and his handsome wife. Charlie was a retired gamekeeper who had served in the Suffolk Regiment in the First War in France and miraculously survived. He had a full greying beard, brown eyes and wore brown corduroy plus-fours and jacket with a moleskin waistcoat, and sat in an upright armchair contentedly puffing a clay pipe. He skinned and stuffed birds beautifully. I remember a pair of turtle-doves on his windowsill. He spoke with a soft East Suffolk lilt about the trials and rewards of his profession of which he was a master, and the past great shooting days. He was a grey partridge-rearing and driving expert and remembered the days when Ely Quilter, using two guns, would usually shoot four birds out of each driven covey. Charles's son Ben was gamekeeper at Foxboro'. He worked from a large hut in the woods, full of rabbit traps and nets and bags of pheasant food. He smoked strong, seductive-smelling pipe tobacco called Honey Dew rolled into cigarettes. He knew where the game was. He would look at his watch and say, 'If we go now there will be a covey of partridges feeding in the corner of the Pond Field.' He was invariably right. It was Ben who taught me to work ferrets, flight duck on the River Deben and shoot rabbits; he introduced me to the ways and beauty of the countryside.

My grandfather George Sutherland died in 1937 when I was sixteen and my father, who was running Begg Roberts and Co in London, began to spend time at Cringletie with Joan and the children. I joined them during Eton holidays. I thought Joan bright, positive and fun, playing golf and tennis and shooting grouse. We got on well. With her sophisticated style and attractive manner, Joan ran a marvellous house at Cringletie in the 1930s with delicious food. There was the mouth-watering smell of young grouse slowly roasting on a bed of wild thyme. She knew how to spend my father's money and give everyone a good time. Most of the hills and uplands in the district were heather-covered and grouse were far more important than sheep. The key people on the moors were gamekeepers and their dogs, with heather preservation their main task. John McKellar, intelligent and reliable, served in the Cameron Highlanders in France in the First War. In his thirties he lived in a comfortable cottage built for him and his wife by my grandfather on the edge of the North Slipperfield grouse moor in the Pentland Hills ten miles from Cringletie. By common consent McKellar was one of the great producers and drivers of grouse in all weathers in the Borders in his day. He would say in his lilting Invernesshire accent and with military precision, 'Today we have a high west wind. In this drive I want the beaters well forward on the right and three flankers hidden to turn the birds downhill over the guns and three men behind with dogs to pick up.' There were many memorable driven grouse days using double guns, never to be repeated, the best, 605 grouse on 15 August, 1933. My father had a good natural eye. An Eton fives champion and tennis player in his youth, he was an excellent driven game shot in spite of losing a leg. We had a lot of fun shooting together over the years. From John McKellar I learned to appreciate the ways and spectacular changing beauty of the moors and uplands, the grouse's contented call and the curlew's lonely cry.

At Eton I followed my father's advice and aimed myself

towards Sandhurst and, if possible, the Black Watch. This meant doing as well as I could in the Officers' Training Corps and passing the Army Entrance Exam. There were plenty of depressing noises coming from Germany and Hitler. Arthur Huson joined us filling sandbags to protect the windows of Wotton House against enemy bombers. 'This could seriously interfere with our cricket,' he bemoaned.

I cycled over to RAF Heston to watch Neville Chamberlain, the PM, and Alec Douglas Home, his PPS, fly in from Germany in a twin-engined plane and land on the bumpy grass field. We crowded round to see the PM wave a piece of paper with a message from Hitler and say, 'This is peace in our time'. For an impressionable schoolboy of seventeen this was heady stuff. Cycling back with Kenneth Sutherland, we felt a bit reassured by the PM. Little did we realize that the egregious Hitler was taking us all for a ride.

There were some hilarious Corps Field Days when, dressed in a buff-coloured military tunic with Eton Blue stripes, plus-fours, hob-nailed boots and long puttees and carrying a .303 rifle, we drilled in desultory manner and moved around the countryside aimlessly. At the end of the summer term there was a 10-day Corps camp. This was a bit better organized; one slept in a bell tent, but a coloured flag represented the light machine gun we were supposed to have. During the 1938 camp in the Aldershot training area I was trying to hide myself in a ditch, which the exercise required, when a marvellous-looking figure suddenly cantered by, dressed in well-cut Black Watch tartan breeches, black riding boots, cut-away khaki jacket, polished Sam Browne belt, Glengarry, and glass monocle clamped in the eye. Soaking wet, I slowly clambered to my feet, holding my mud-encrusted rifle, and shouted, 'Buzz off'. It was Captain Bernard Fergusson, then French Instructor at Sandhurst!

In October, 1938, I sat and passed the Army Entrance Exam.

2

Sandhurst, The Black Watch and Dunkirk

1939–40

In the 1930s the Sandhurst course lasted 18 months, three terms of 6 months. There were two colleges, Old and New. When I became a gentleman cadet in New College in January, 1939, the full long-established course was in place. We were on the go from 6 am to 10 pm. It was a culture shock. Much emphasis was laid on high standards of personal turnout and dress. Hours were spent cleaning and polishing one's boots, rifle and bayonet scabbard, using Kiwi polish, water and methylated spirit till one could see the reflection of one's face. Luckily I had Mr Deacon, one of the best New College servants, to help me pass the Junior Under Officers' inspection. There were endless periods of drill with a group of senior Brigade of Guards drill sergeants, faces contorted in fury, barking unintelligible orders to knock us into shape. 'You are a dozy gentleman Mr Sutherland,' was a familiar parade-ground cry. 'Put him in the book,' was another. Thus my name was written in the drill sergeant's book and I had an extra 15 minutes' torture.

One quickly got the message. There was tactical work in the classroom and time spent on army organization and administration and studying the manual *Imperial Policing*. Outdoors we did rangework, equitation, driving trucks and motor-cycles and a lot of PT and games, which I enjoyed. I recall pounding wearily round the Oak Grove running track to hear a voice shouting, 'Well run Sutherland, you'll be very good in a retreat.' I looked round and there stood a distinguished-looking figure dressed in a tweed suit wearing a brown hat. It was Bernard Fergusson. Next time round the track I stopped and said, 'Sir, you don't really mean that do you?' With monocle in eye he replied, 'Perhaps'. Strange and prophetic, as within the year I was in the Dunkirk Débâcle.

There were two Black Watch captains on the Sandhurst staff, Bernard Fergusson teaching French and Noel Roper Caldbeck teaching general subjects and keeping an eye on cadet aspirants for the Regiment. Roper Caldbeck was a great Black Watch figure, having won the Sword of Honour at Sandhurst some years before. He lived at the charming Oak Grove House with his beautiful wife. I was invited several times to dine there, always a pleasure to enjoy the calm and escape the noise of New College.

The key moment in the progress towards one's commissioning is the interview with the Colonel of the Regiment. General Sir Mark Cameron was one of the most distinguished Colonels the Black Watch has had. We talked alone for 20 minutes in a room in Old College. It was mid-May, 1939. He asked why I wanted to join the Black Watch. I quoted my family connection, which he knew all about. He asked what my general interests were. I told him about my life in Suffolk and Scotland. He was austere and intimidating. After lunch I decided to take the rest of the day off and go up to London. As the London train was about to leave Camberley Station, I flung my bike into a rack, headed for the nearest carriage and just made a seat in the corner. In the opposite corner was a figure hidden behind *The Times*. This was General Cameron. We talked about the Nazi threat, the worsening international situation, and Gibraltar, where he had been Governor. We got on well.

In the 1930s most of the top dozen young men passing out of Sandhurst went into the Indian Army. The pay and promotion prospects were good and they had the interest and excitement of a lifetime of 'serious soldiering' in the Indian sub-continent. There was also the glamour of fabulous looking uniforms and romantic-sounding Regimental names. I recall the evening when a young officer in the Indian Cavalry came and sat next to me at dinner in New College mess. He wore a beautiful dark blue mess jacket with a red lining, a row of small gold buttons on the edges, and a heavily gold-embroidered waistcoat. He was, I believe, in the Poonah Horse. I mention this because two years later, in 1941, I was in No 8 Commando attached to 18th Indian Cavalry. When it came to fieldcraft, movement and observation in desert conditions, they knew it all. We were simply not in the same league.

For me the summer of 1939 was a time of memorable fun with plenty of fabulous big band, white tie and tails dances, lots of pretty girls, masses of champagne and delicious food. We did not allow the darkening threats from Germany to intrude on or spoil our fun. On 20 August I had to break my holiday in Scotland and return abruptly to Sandhurst to find that all the cadets in the two forms senior to me had been commissioned and left. I was now a senior and a sergeant in charge of a cadet platoon. A few new officers appeared on the staff, but the training remained more or less unchanged. I was sitting at a table in a New College Hall of Study to hear Mr Chamberlain declare war on the radio in his flat, depressing, unconvincing voice. It was 3 September, 1939. He seemed an old, tired and dejected man. We were all speculating on how this dire news might affect our lives when the air-raid warning siren sounded. We walked to some trenches dug in the ground behind New College and waited there for the All Clear, which came quickly. Some of the time during my last month at Sandhurst was spent digging trenches, 1914–1918 war style, using the army pick, spade and shovel. Two experts were produced to show us how to do it. Time was also spent on map reading and compass work. This was useful later on in France. There was great pressure to get rid of us quickly and use the valuable Sandhurst officer-training space for newcomers. I remember my last RSM's parade. RSM Brand, formerly of the Grenadier Guards, was the senior and most influential Warrant Officer in the Army. To us cadets he was 'God'. On his order 'March on the College' there was a squeak of wheels on gravel as a station porter's barrow holding an enormous book appeared. It moved to the centre of the parade, halting in front of the RSM. Whereupon the cadet holding the book released a cadet hidden inside and gave the RSM an immaculate salute. We were all watching the RSM's reaction to this hilarious scene. The distinguished, slightly portly figure, with his pace-stick under his arm, roared with laughter.

On 22 October, 1939 (one week before my nineteenth birthday) I left Sandhurst and was commissioned into the Black Watch. Fortunately, I have had two periods in my life at Sandhurst, nine months in 1939 as a harassed cadet when one was working against time and totally at the receiving end, and three years in the early 1950s as an instructor, when the tempo was more relaxed and one tried to influence a bit the nature, content and direction of the leadership course there.

My father was pleased I was following his footsteps. When I was at Cringletie at the end of October there were two regimental ties for me with a short, congratulatory note from him. One was the Black Watch, the dark blue and green of the 42nd tartan with a bold red stripe, the other the mauve and purple of the Highland Brigade. Apparently these are the colours of the ubiquitous and indestructible Scottish thistle!

In those days when much of the world's map was coloured 'Red', each infantry regiment had two battalions, one at home, the other overseas. In 1939, 1st Battalion Black Watch was at Dover, the other in Palestine. I was posted to the Depot at Queen's Barracks, Perth, at the heart of the Black Watch recruiting area. Commanding the Depot was Colonel Vesey Holt, a contemporary of my father, the red-faced, chain-smoking hero of several First World War battles. I remember him turning to me and saying, 'David, I am now about to give you your first order in the Regiment. Tomorrow morning 9.15 outside the Officers' Mess, one gun, one bag of cartridges. You are shooting with Lord Mansfield and if you miss anything you'll never be asked again.' I wasn't!

The soldiers were quartered in the desperately cold Perth Dye Works, the officers like me in various hotels. Some well-known Black Watch and Perthshire names appeared, Bowes Lyon, Cox, Orr Ewing, Drummond. We did some desultory trench digging near Scone Palace Racecourse, and quaint bayonet fighting on the barrack square. Life was easy and unhurried. We fed in the Officers' mess, that low, mellow-coloured Georgian cavalry barracks where Mr Semple, the steward, attended to our mid-morning needs of port and plum cake.

Shortly after the war began in September, 1939, a large British Expeditionary Force started to take up defensive positions facing Germany along the line of the frontier between France and Belgium. In February, 1940, I was posted as a platoon commander in 6th Battalion Black Watch in 4 Infantry Division, BEF. I was in charge of a small draft of reinforcements for 6th Black Watch. There were no pipes and drums to play us clear of Dover harbour and no 'Black Bear', the evocative, stirring, traditional march for Highland troops embarking for service overseas. But there was a young 6th Battalion piper on board and at my request he played 'The High Road to Linton' in fine style. Everyone wore battledress: an easy-fitting khaki blouse and thick trousers with a large pocket in the left leg. This intelligently designed clothing was in use throughout the war and for many years afterwards. In our bonnets we wore the Red Hackle. By government order the kilt had just been withdrawn from Highland Regiments on the grounds that it made us 'conspicuous'. There was a huge row about this. From 1941 onwards in the Middle East I wore the 42 tartan kilt on all possible occasions. The slow train took us to Mouroux, near Lille, and the distinctive acrid smell of French tobacco reminded me that I was abroad for the first time in my life.

The battalion was commanded by Lieutenant-Colonel Garry Carthew Yorkston who next day welcomed me in his office. I noticed he had the First World War medals and he said he wanted me to join 'C' Company which was commanded by Major Berowald Innes. It was a bit of luck for me as he was from Perth and a well-known Black Watch family. Berowald Innes got up to welcome me. We talked about the extraordinarily long and extremely cold winter in France, and how 6 Black Watch, part of 4 Division, were in reserve.

The 4 Division sign was an orange with a quarter cut out. We wore this on our battledress sleeves. Above this we wore the ribbon of the French Croix de Guerre which had been awarded to the battalion in the First World War.

This was the period of the 'phoney war', when there was little or no activity on either side and we thought the war would end soon because the French defences of the Maginot Line were too strong to be taken by the Germans. How mistaken we were.

Berowald Innes told me to go to 12 Platoon as its Commander. The Platoon Sergeant of the platoon was John McVey, a lively man with a weatherbeaten face who worked in the building trade in Perth. He was old enough to be my father and also had First World War medals. When it came to trench-digging and using the resources of the countryside to keep one going he had no equal. We spent our time on route marches and digging and preparing trenches 1914–1918 style, using wooden A-frames. We had a Brigade trench-digging competition where depth, parapet and parados had to be exact. I felt 12 Platoon had won, so did John McVey, but no. And so the long, bitter winter of storms, ice and snow gradually gave way to the green fields, woods and poplar trees of spring.

During the night of 9/10 May, when I was Battalion Duty Officer, the telephone rang. A sepulchral voice at Brigade HQ said, 'The Germans have invaded the Low Countries.' I could not believe my ears, and thought, 'What on earth can we do?' The attack was completely unexpected and caught us off guard. There was a plan which involved moving troops into Belgium to meet the German attack. 4 Division was a Reserve Division and not due to move into Belgium at once. I remember being told to pack my personal kit in a suitcase and leave it in a dump at the officer's mess. I never saw it again. A pity, as my radio would have been useful to get news from the BBC. After much sitting around and waiting, on the night of 13 May we began to move to Brussels in troop carriers. I sat next to the driver of one, John McVey in another. The platoon had twenty-two men. We went through Brussels in daylight and I remember pretty girls giving us flowers. 'So far so good,' I said to myself. We dug in on the line of the Vilvorde Canal on 17 May. This was a major tank obstacle some 200 metres wide. John McVey and I discussed where the weapon pits should be positioned. During the day 3rd Division passed through us, retiring from Louvain, and the bridge over the canal was blown. Shortly afterwards, during the night, the enemy came up to the canal and I could spot them moving about clearly with my binoculars. I sent a written message to Berowald Innes about this by runner. We had no wireless communications. The enemy also began shelling behind our position. Next day, 18 May, we were ordered to withdraw.

We marched some 30 miles to positions behind the River Dendre, a long and exhausting march in the hot summer sun, which took all day but was unhindered by the enemy. The road was crowded with refugees streaming out of Brussels which had just been taken by the Germans. Once across the Dendre the bridge was blown. I remember sitting, footsore, beside the road under a tree with my boots in the air to restore the circulation in my feet, taking long gulps of water from my water-bottle, when the admirable John McVey came up to report. All 12 Platoon men had made it, but had foot blisters. I had a chat with Berowald Innes; he looked tired and exhausted. We both felt terribly demoralized. Shortly afterwards he was wounded at Oudenarde.

There was a good meal of soup, stewed potatoes and tinned peaches to stem our hunger. We waited for troop transport and were taken to positions behind the River Escaut where we were held in reserve for two days. The Germans crossed the Escaut on 22 May, punching a hole on 4 Division's left. Next day we had to repair the damage by pushing the Germans back. As we started to move forward the Germans began to move round our left, using numerous well-placed machine guns and heavy shelling to pin us down. To make matters worse, we had no communications whatever. This was a terrible day. By dusk I had seven casualties in the platoon – four dead and three wounded including John McVey, hit in the shoulder, who ended the war a prisoner. Then I had a welcome message by runner to march to Halluin. There were ten men in the platoon. Behind me was Lance-Corporal John Walker, a miner from Keltie in Fife, and eight men. We were exhausted, so I said, 'Let's sleep for two hours before we begin.' We collapsed in a barn beside the road. Men from the battalion and other units marched by. As we approached the village of Sweveghem, people said, 'Watch out for German snipers.' I was interested in enemy activity three miles to the east, where some horse-drawn wagons pulling observation balloons were moving in the same direction as we were. I was looking over a wall using my binoculars, John Walker beside me. There was an appalling crack, clouds of cement dust, and John Walker was on his back on the road, blood pouring from his throat. Mercifully he did not die. The thickness of the cement wall saved him. We quickly got him on a passing truck to be taken for medical attention. I thought to myself, 'You have had a miraculous escape; never again take such liberties with the

Germans.' I picked up John Walker's rifle and threw away the uncomfortable and conspicuous steel helmet in favour of the soft tam o'shanter and red hackle.

We reached Halluin, a focal point on the Franco-Belgian frontier, during the night of 25 May. We marched through an abandoned building site: concrete mixers, steel reinforcing bars and bags of cement, which I took to be the unfinished northern end of the Maginot Line. The Germans knew all about, and used to their advantage, the large gap in Allied defences. On 25 May the BBC reported that the Germans were in Boulogne. Having no radio set, I missed this abysmal news, probably just as well. From Halluin we marched west for about five miles and waited, facing east, at Comines, which is just south of the Lys Canal. I now had no effective map. The invaluable sheet which served me well on the road from Brussels ended at Halluin. I never got another.

On the night of 27 May we heard that the Germans were striking westwards towards Messines on the north side of the Lys Canal. The battalion had to move quickly to get as many men as possible over Warneton Bridge to intercept the German move. There was a spirited daylight counter-attack by 'A' Company supported by armoured cars of the 13th/18th Hussars which held the Germans off. Once all troops were across the Warneton Bridge it was blown. I remember spending the night of 28 May dug in facing the Germans: they left us alone.

Next day elements of 5 Division and other units passed through us and we became the honourable but unenviable rearguard. The following day came the order to disengage from the enemy after dark and rendezvous with the battalion transport, which had been hidden in the woods near Ploegsteert. I found it difficult to disengage my six men quickly, and so missed the 11 pm pick-up. We arrived at the main crossroads in Messines and found it empty. This presented a bit of a problem. None of us knew where the battalion had gone and I had no map. It was now about midnight and

Messines shut tight for the night. The senior man in 12 Platoon was Francis Watson, a shepherd from Aberfeldy. I said to him, 'You stay here with the others and rest and I will take the main road to the north and see if I can see any Germans.' Before long I saw some distinctive white flares hovering in the air about two miles away, indicating the Germans were there. I walked back to Messines and reported to the men. It was 2 am. We felt that by walking at night and sleeping by day we had less chance of meeting the enemy. We left Messines by a westerly road and walked till dawn, sleeping next day in a large wood. We had seen no enemy and so continued on the same road, in the same direction, the next night. At about 4 am we were quietly going through a small village when I saw a farm wagon in the middle of the road ahead, a cockney voice demanding, 'Who are you? Give the password,' and the sound of rifles being cocked. I stopped and replied, 'I do not know the password but we are Black Watch. Let us pass.' They were a Middlesex Regiment team manning a road block. 'You are the last to come through as we are leaving in 4 hours' time for Dunkirk.' This was the first time I learned where our destination was. I could not believe that our defeat was so rapid and so devastating.

The sergeant in charge of the road block offered a truck to take us to Fournes, near La Panne, which I accepted with real gratitude. At Fournes there were roads full of refugees, men, women and children coming from Belgium with all their possessions packed on horsedrawn carts. There were plenty of French soldiers milling around not knowing where to go or what to do. There was an elderly French Corporal releasing pigeons from a mobile loft. Perhaps there was no more need for them to carry messages or their food had run out! Most flew back to the dejected-looking Corporal and went on perching on the loft's roof. A few took off and soared upwards into the clear blue sky and disappeared. I wondered, at the time, if these pigeons, in some strange way, might represent the destiny of France – the stodgy majority staying put under German occupation and the courageous few flying away to return later as liberators.

The seven of us walked slowly through the sand dunes to La Panne. On the way we passed elements of the battalion dug in behind the Nieuport Road covering the beaches' approaches. There was no enemy air or ground activity near us, but Dunkirk, five miles away, was being heavily shelled and bombed from the air and in flames. Battalion Head-quarters was a small room dug deep into the sand dunes at La Panne. The Colonel, looking exhausted, came out to greet me and wanted to know the details of my journey back from Messines. I said I had been lucky taking the right road. He agreed. He went on to mention the number of key officers and NCOs we had lost and the need to rebuild the battalion as soon as possible after we got back to England. He told me about Berowald Innes' wound, which I knew about, and Robert Orr Ewing's death, which I did not. He said, 'I would like you to return to England tomorrow and be ready with others to help me re-train the new 6th Battalion Black Watch as soon as it is re-formed.' The idea seemed irresistible to me and he was the kind of man I respected and with whom I could work closely. At this point Brian Madden, the highly efficient adjutant, appeared and we arranged that I should leave on 1st June.

I remember my last night in La Panne. There was a reassuring Officers' Mess hamper filled with 'goodies' that had somehow survived the difficult journey. With Brian Madden I finished off an excellent bottle of vintage port as we discussed the trials and tribulations of the retreat. As ordered, I threw my rifle on the large pile of weapons on the beach and, with many others, walked through the shallows towards a Royal Navy gunboat. It was 11 am, flat calm, blazing sun. I got into an approaching small naval cutter and was rowed about 400 metres and deposited on the gunboat, where I said one prayer to the Almighty, the other to the Royal Navy, and slept for five hours. The ship was bombed but mercifully not hit. I landed at Folkestone Harbour. Two days later, Colonel Carthew Yorkston was on a destroyer which was heavily bombed and he was wounded. So, sadly, he did not return to command the 6th Battalion Black Watch.

For me the short Flanders Campaign of May, 1940, had some stark and bitter lessons. We had been completely out-fought and out-manoeuvred by the Germans. This was because we had completely different concepts of how the war should be fought. They had long-prepared plans involving machine guns, artillery, tanks and aircraft working together in a mobile role. We had linear defence 1914–1918 war style with communications to match. From this I deduced we would have completely to reorganize and re-train our army before we could take on the Germans again on land. This would take several years (it took four years). These were my personal thoughts. I learned more on that ghastly three-week retreat in May, 1940, than at any time in my life. How thin is the thread between life and death. What a special privilege it is to lead good men into and out of battle. How formidable the German war machine was and how difficult to defeat. I was a lucky 2nd Lieutenant of nineteen.

3

Joining the Commandos

1940

Every family in the land had one or more of its men in France and the anxiety during that June week was intense. As the tea-ladies came down the train before it left for Winchester, one could tell from their faces whether their man was back or not. It is nothing short of a miracle that 235,000 British and 113,000 Allied troops returned to fight another day. Winchester is the Rifle Brigade depot and I walked from the station to the barracks carrying a small haversack slung over my shoulder. By chance I discovered that the depot was commanded by Colonel Rhys Mansell, an old friend of my father. He was astonished and relieved to see me and kindly offered his telephone for me to tell my parents I was safely back, which I happily did. They were delighted. After a most comfortable night, a much-needed hot bath and wearing borrowed clothes, next morning I set off for Maiden Newton in Dorset, where 6th Battalion Black Watch was being re-formed. Maiden Newton is a quiet hamlet set deep in rural Dorset six miles from the sea. For the first time we brought the disturbance of the war to their doorstep, but they were helpful and co-operative. The mood in the country was depressed and sombre. We were bracing ourselves for a German invasion by sea with paratroops dropping on targets inland. Then came that masterly radio address from Winston Churchill in his deep gravelly voice, giving us and the world the clear twin messages of defiance and hope. That did a lot to restore national morale. The reinforcements for Black Watch came from the Staffordshire Regiment. We had to humour them a bit before they would exchange their old, traditional regimental headgear for our tam-o'-shanter and red hackle. We had a large contingent of new rifles from Canada on which to train, which kept us all busy. As troops were needed at once to man defences on the South Coast I was sent to reconnoitre positions near Portland Bill, which we occupied day and night, looking gloomily out to sea.

★ ★ ★

On 3 June, 1940, Winston Churchill, now PM, was concerned that an offensive spirit must be fostered. He wrote to the Chiefs of Staff to 'propose measures for a vigorous, enterprising and ceaseless offensive against the whole German occupied coastline'. This requirement was handled by the PA to the CIGS, Lieutenant-Colonel Dudley Clarke of the Royal Artillery. The aim was to form and train a volunteer force of about 5,000. Clarke, a guerrilla warfare expert with experience in the Arab revolt in Palestine, thought the new forces should be named after the Boer Commandos who had given us so much trouble and tied down so many British troops during the South African War of 1899–1902. Churchill liked the idea, remembering his own lively encounter with Boer Commandos when he was a war correspondent during the South African war. The Commandos derailed an armoured train Churchill was travelling on and captured him. He later escaped, but ever after admired the Commandos for their courage and skill at arms. So the name 'Commando' stuck. The next move was to start to find the officers and men needed and for this purpose the various military commands within the United Kingdom were made responsible for forming Commandos from the troops under their command.

While this secret planning activity was going on in Whitehall, 6 Black Watch were ordered to move from Maiden

26

Newton to the Isle of Wight. I was the only surviving officer in 'C' Company and at that time the battalion was commanded by Keir Wedderburn, a senior Major in the Regiment who had been old enough to serve in the 1914–1918 war, and later was Adjutant of 1st Battalion. In the Isle of Wight our task was to defend the island against German sea and parachute attacks. Battalion HQ was in Newport and the four Companies each had a bit of the coast to defend. 'C' Company had the area just south of Bembridge – Sandown Bay. I recall getting my platoon to dig in at the designated spot. Some were Staffordshire miners so this was a familiar task. As there was not much to do in the evenings, I used to go and have a drink and a chat with Keir Wedderburn in a comfortable house which had been requisitioned in Newport. We talked about my Dunkirk experiences and what might lie ahead for the country. The Battle of Britain between the RAF and the Luftwaffe had begun in earnest and air dogfights over the Isle of Wight took place daily. Every now and then a German or a British fighter crashed into the sea, the pilot having ejected to safety. Our dull, monotonous routine was: night, awake watching the sea approaches, breakfast, sleep during the day.

After breakfast one morning a despatch rider appeared with a message from the CO. 'Sutherland, I have a couple of letters you should see.' I read the two War Office letters, one calling for volunteers to be trained as parachutists, the other to be trained for raiding tasks in enemy territory. I thought parachuting too dangerous, but the opportunity to join a raiding force might provide the change, excitement and additional responsibility I felt I needed at that moment. So I asked Keir Wedderburn kindly to answer on those lines. Before long a letter arrived calling me for an interview at Sherborne in Dorset. I drove there on an ancient army motorbike, crossing by the Ryde ferry on a glorious sunny day, wondering what might lie ahead for me. Waiting for me to appear was a thick-set man in his mid-thirties with a keen, professional manner, in the uniform of a Lieutenant-Colonel in the Royal Artillery. He introduced himself as John Durnford-Slater. He had just been appointed to command 3 Commando with a strength of 500 men and was looking for volunteers. He asked if I could swim and handle small boats, and why I wanted to join. I told him of my Dunkirk experience and my wish to get into a unit that was active, exciting and with a new task. We got on well and had a cup of tea before I left on my decrepit bike for the Isle of Wight. A few days later I had a letter telling me to report to 3 Commando at Plymouth. Before leaving, I bade my platoon and Keir Wedderburn goodbye.

At Plymouth I met several kindred spirits, such as Peter Young. As for training, I remember, with eleven others, rowing a naval cutter slowly across Plymouth Harbour with a weatherbeaten-faced coxswain swearing at our puerile incompetence. There were some load-carrying marches on Dartmoor, but no one seemed to know what we were supposed to be training for. This soon changed.

In July I went on a 3-week Commando training course at Inverailort Castle on the west coast of Inverness near Mallaig. A large old Highland shooting lodge belonging to the Cameron-Head family had been requisitioned, together with several thousand acres of testing hill for special training. This was Lord Lovat's brainchild. I remember what a romantic figure he was, standing on the lawn in front of the lodge with Lovat Scouts bonnet, battledress, hill-walking boots and stick, with a stalker's telescope in a leather case slung over one shoulder. 'This,' I said to myself, 'must be game, set and match!'

There were plenty of red deer on the property which we could stalk under the keen eye of one of Lord Lovat's men, but not shoot. The trick is patience; keep still, observe an area of ground and wait for the deer to move, as they always will. You can then plan your stalk, taking ground undulations and wind direction into account. If you move too soon yourself, the deer will spot you and disappear. The same applies to the enemy, who always moves, in my experience. If you see him first you have the initiative and can to some extent control events. If the enemy sees you first, you could be in trouble. It follows that the most important item of one's operational equipment was 6 x 30 binoculars.

There were some memorable instructors assembled for the course. Former Shanghai policemen Fairbairn and Sykes, the ugliest pair I have ever seen, gave us unarmed combat in a hilarious, laid-back way. Lieutenant-Colonel Grant Taylor, a famous pistol shot, taught us to nail a playing card at 20 paces! There were many day and night exercises using landing craft in the sheltered waters of nearby Loch Ailort, and others further out to sea, and many stiff marches bearing heavy loads. To me each day was interesting and fun, and each night in a bell tent on the lawn I slept like a log.

Life-enhancers are rare people. They have that infectious *joie de vivre*. Over the years I have met two. It soon got around that the Rifle Brigade Captain who looked like David Niven really was the debonair charmer himself. The mail was delivered each Wednesday. We all crowded round to see who got what. For Niven there was a huge coloured postcard of a fantastic Californian palm-fringed beach, and the message: 'David, what are you doing over there? Come back soon, love Ginger.' Ginger Rogers was the prettiest, funniest lady in Hollywood and a great dancer! The next Wednesday there was a bulky envelope for David Niven. This contained a splendid blue woollen comforter for one's private person. 'I'm glad to have this,' David Niven remarked, 'it will keep me warm during the approaching winter. The funny thing is that these interesting things are knitted by an old spinster friend of mine in Memphis, Tennessee, and she doesn't know what they are for!'

The food was not particularly good, so on the last evening of the course David Niven booked a large table at the local pub. We had spinach soup, grilled salmon, raspberries and cream. The owner had an attractive daughter who kept peeping at David Niven through the kitchen door. He could take this no longer. He stormed into the kitchen and kissed her: she fainted. I remember David Niven saying to the flabbergasted proprietor, 'Sir, you will have to put some backbone into this pretty girl before I take her on as a leading lady!'

On my way back to 3 Commando at Plymouth I remember having a good grouse shoot in Peeblesshire with my father, 500 birds in a week. Little did I know that it would be five years before I shot grouse again. In September, 1940, 3 Commando moved to Scotland for mountain and landing-craft training. Based at Inveraray, we exercised day and night on the Duke of Argyll's steep hills and deep forests above Loch Fyne. Two months earlier, 3 Commando had undertaken an abortive night raid against the German defences in Guernsey. Many lessons were learnt, including the need to increase the strength of the Commando troop from three officers and forty-seven men to four officers and sixty men, so each troop could fit into two landing craft. With ten troops, 3 Commando was now 600 men and forty officers. We were now getting more proficient at using landing-craft and men to cross a beach quickly, attack a target inland and re-embark under counter-attack.

The arrival of three large, specially converted, fast cargo ships, the *Glen Roy*, the *Glen Erne* and the *Glen Gyle*, raised our morale. These big ships each carried a dozen landing-craft. I remember being told that the Chief of Combined Operations, Admiral Sir Roger Keyes, was to address us. There was silence on the ship when the old Admiral was piped aboard. Then, leaning on the ship's rail, an alert, weather-beaten-faced figure appeared with gold braid up to his elbows and medals to match. In a commanding voice the First War Zeebrugge Raid hero said, 'Men, you have worked hard and deserve a rest. I am going to send you on ten days' leave, and when you return we will embark on an enterprise that will stir the world,' and disappeared. For 2nd Lieutenant David Sutherland of No. 3 troop, looking up from the bowels of *Glen Roy*, this was heady stuff.

I remember having an excellent leave in Suffolk and Peeblesshire, wondering what lay ahead. As the operation was delayed, we moved to billets in Largs on the Ayrshire coast. There was insufficient work for the 3 Commando explosives people, so they asked if they could fell a large tree near Lord Glasgow's house. They over-estimated the amount of explosive needed, smashed many windows and left the unfortunate Peer trapped in the lavatory, furiously screaming, 'When will these terrible people go away?' Evelyn Waugh, in *Officers and Gentlemen*, covers this hilarious scene.

There was a final full-scale rehearsal for the landing by 3 Commando and 8 Commando which was to take place near Brodrick on the Island of Arran. On the efficiency and dash of that rehearsal the fate of the operation depended. To watch the rehearsal, Admiral Keyes sent a party of great men I assumed to be the VCIGS, VCDS and a member of Churchill's Cabinet. The date chosen was 15 December, 1940. At 2 pm Colonel Durnford-Slater called an 'O' group at which he gave the officers their orders for the final rehearsal. We were sitting in the wardroom, the only place in the ship large enough to hold us all. I was in the front taking notes. In his striking, confident voice, John Durnford-Slater spoke in detail for 20 minutes without notes about our task, and how vital it was for the country and the Commandos' future for the enterprise to succeed. 'We may never have another chance,' I remember him saying. 'Remember, Guernsey was a failure.' He then turned to the question of timing. 'Leading troops must be on the beach at 2 am precisely. Allowing time for waking up, putting on battle kit and getting into the landing-craft, plus 20 minutes to reach the beach, this means we must all have an early call at 1 am. Little sleep tonight, but there it is. Now, who shall we have to call us?' For some reason fifty pairs of eyes turned towards me, I suppose because I was young, keen and fit and sitting in front. So I spoke to my batman, Lance Corporal Fuller, DCLI, and told him to rouse me at 1 am, had a light supper in the wardroom and went fast asleep in my cabin. There are times in one's life when, being anxious and bone tired, one sleeps like the dead. That was such a night. It took ten seconds of arm-shaking and loud shouting in my ear by Fuller before I surfaced. 'It's 1.45, you must get up, sir.'

It was one of the few times in my life when total panic in my mind and body took over. I was horrified that we were going to be seriously late. Everyone was cursing at the sudden inconvenience of trying to put on battledress, boots and helmet in a hurry in the dark. I got my men stirring but forgot to take some important TSMG magazines with me. It was bedlam as organization broke down and each man tried to get on the nearest landing-craft. I groaned, looking back at the *Glen Roy* from about 100 yards to see some of my men still lining her rails. The landing-craft struck the beach on time but the follow-up was chaotic. For the three wise men, that landing was an anti-climax. They had had enough, standing around stamping their feet emptying their whisky flasks on a cold December night, waiting for us to turn up. They told Admiral Keyes that his men were not ready for an operation of this kind. For Colonel John Durnford-Slater this was a body blow. In my varied professional life I have had several serious rockets but none as telling or deserved as this. He was beside himself with rage and slowly, clinically, over ten minutes verbally tore me apart for oversleeping. In reply I said I was deeply sorry for having let him and everyone else down so badly, and that this would never happen again. As a measure of regimental concern, I was given by Captain Charles Head, the Adjutant, 21 days' duty officer, starting at once, which prevented me taking leave over Christmas.

There is an interesting sequel to my monumental *gaffe*. After the war, in October, 1945, when Robert Laycock was now a General and Chief of Combined Operations, he sent for me to come to his office at Richmond House, Whitehall. We greeted each other warmly. Last time I had seen him was in a Cairo hospital bed 2 years earlier when he was recovering from the Rommel Raid. Then he was a haggard shell of a man weighing about 8 stone, now once more alert, bright, fit and 10-stone-plus. I congratulated him on his promotion and remarkable recovery. He said, 'David, do you remember the time when you overslept on the Commando exercise rehearsal in Scotland in December, 1940?' 'General,' I replied, 'I will never forget it!' He continued, 'Did you know our destination?' I replied, 'No, that was top secret. I remember you asked me to look at a stereo pair of photographs showing a lot of stone walls and olive trees.' He continued, 'That was the Italian island of Pantelleria, our objective. It lay 200 miles to the west of Malta midway between Sicily and Tunisia. There was a large Italian garrison and, because the Commando operation had been delayed twice, we now know that the Italians knew about our plan to attack Pantelleria and were ready for us. If the attack had gone ahead it would have been a catastrophe. The two Glen ships would have had to face German submarines and attack from the Luftwaffe and Italian air force, and if No 3 and No 8 Commandos managed to land on Pantelleria we would have had a furious battle on our hands, with many killed and wounded and prisoners-of-war. By oversleeping you did us all a good turn.'

At this point, I remember, the General produced a bottle of gin and we had a huge gin and tonic together to celebrate his promotion and our lucky deliverance. Naturally one is not so pretentious as to believe that one very junior officer oversleeping in 1940 affected the course of the war. But it could have had a dramatic and disastrous effect on the history and fortunes of the Commandos and the SAS. It would have been terrible if all the officers and men of 3 and 8 Commandos and two Commando ships had been eliminated for good at that early stage in the war. Some important and able Commando leaders would have disappeared, such as John Durnford-Slater and Peter Young in No 3 and Robert Laycock in No 8. The SAS would not have existed, as David Stirling and the 'originals', those marvellous and intrepid characters Pat Riley, Jim Almonds, Ernie Bond, Bob Bennett and others, were in No 8. There must be a moral behind this extraordinary story. Every now and then, to this day, I say a prayer to *le bon Dieu* for letting me oversleep on that fateful night long ago and so, with many others, escape the deadly jaws of the Pantelleria trap!

4

With 18th Indian Cavalry in Tobruk

July–September, 1941

Since my oversleeping had successfully killed off the operation for which all of us had been training furiously for months, Whitehall planners and GHQ Middle East decided there was a need for a Commando force in the Middle East to capture the island of Rhodes. As the duty officer, confined to *Glen Roy* carrying out the remainder of Colonel Durnford-Slater's sentence, I soon discovered that we were shortly sailing 'overseas'. Interesting-looking crates bulging with tropical clothing and 'pith helmets' were loaded on board. Only one troop of 3 Commando, commanded by Michael Kealy, was to go to the Middle East, the remainder staying at home. I wangled my way into Kealy's troop by taking the place of John Pine-Coffin who wanted to remain at home. In this way I changed from No 3 to No 8 Commando. For various reasons this suited me. It would be impossible for me ever to regain John Durnford-Slater's confidence. Serving in the Middle East sounded interesting and new. I had two school friends, Julian Berry and Gavin Astor, in No 8. There was a hectic but memorable ten days' leave split between Foxboro' and Cringletie – a wonderful, warm family send-off. Little did I know that it would be four years before I returned.

On 31 January, 1941, the fast Glen ships *Glen Roy* and *Glen Gyle* sailed from the Isle of Arran. Code-named 'Force

Z', under Lieutenant-Colonel Robert Laycock, were Nos 7, 8 and 11 Commandos, a troop from 3 Commando and Roger Courtney's Folboat Section, a force of 100 officers and 1,500 other ranks. The third Glen ship, *Glen Erne*, followed a few days later with elements of a Mobile Beach Defence organization. Little did we imagine what sagas lay ahead. 'Force Z' was of great importance, so the ships, protected by a cruiser and two destroyers, headed west, deep into the Atlantic, to avoid German submarines. This meant sailing straight into a furious westerly storm. On *Glen Roy* I shared a small cabin with Michael Alexander, he on the bottom bunk, me on the top. Never have I felt so miserable or so seasick. The ship shuddered as she lurched into the next huge wave. Everything had to be battened down. One could see *Glen Gyle* in the distance, propellers turning in the air as she drove through the ugly seas. This continued for five hideous days and nights. As we turned south the weather gradually improved and we sat on the upper decks enjoying the welcome sun.

Glen Roy was full of interesting and engaging people. Robert Laycock had eight troops of 8 Commando under him. Officers and men of the Brigade of Guards were well to the fore, particularly George Jellicoe, Coldstream Guards, Carol Mather and Jock Lewes, Welsh Guards, Tom Langton, Irish Guards, Desmond Buchanan, Grenadier Guards, Philip Dunne, Royal Horse Guards, and David Stirling, Scots Guards. The latter spent much of the night playing *chemin de fer*, and sleeping during the day. There were a number of NCOs including Bob Bennett, Jim Almonds and Pat Riley, who later became prominent and distinguished early members of the SAS. The rumbustious Randolph Churchill was on board, I suspect to provide a link for Robert Laycock to the Prime Minister. Also the irascible Evelyn Waugh, already compiling preliminary thoughts for his 'Sword of Honour' trilogy. To keep an eye on the state of our morale, Sir Roger Keyes sent out an old shipmate, Admiral Sir Walter Cowan. Well into his seventies, this delightful man had been present at most engagements since the Nile expedition of 1898 and was anxious not to miss the next! He walked round the upper deck to keep fit. Now and again I joined him there and we chatted about the forthcoming Rhodes operation.

After a couple of weeks we put into Freetown to take on food and water. It was becoming hot and humid, and one could see palm trees low down in the distance. After we had anchored for about an hour, a small rowing-boat appeared from which stepped a 'poor white' with a Bombay bowler offering to take anyone's laundry, for a moderate sum, and have it skilfully washed, ironed and returned as new. Several Turnbull and Asser heavy silk shirts were handed over, never to be seen again! Around the ship moved a shoal of local fishermen in bark canoes waiting for us to throw down coins into the water which they would then pick up and keep. One of the canoeists spotted the Padre standing alone near the after rail and asked him to throw what he had. For some reason the Padre declined. Then came the earthy rejoinder, 'No money for a poor fisherman, no black woman for you tonight!' There was a spontaneous roar of delight from 500 male voices witnessing the hilarious exchange. To give him his due, the Padre was unmoved by this *exposé*. It was 'business as usual' the next Sunday service.

Conditions on *Glen Roy* were cramped and there was little to do. Boxing matches took place on the after part of the ship. Desmond Buchanan, Douglas Pomford, a Golden Gloves champion, and Cyril Feebury were prominent, and all went on to give distinguished service in the SAS. It is interesting that boxers are both brave and cunning when it comes to war.

After a month at sea we spent two days relaxing in Cape Town. I remember the incredible hospitality shown to us. It was late summer and everything seemed at its best – the grapes and peaches, lobsters at the City Club, sunlit Table Mountain, surfing at Meusenberg, dancing at Kelvin Grove, all was perfection. I said to myself, here is a place one must try to return to one day. We went on past the east coast of Africa, north up the Red Sea to Suez, arriving there on 7 March, 1941. We marched to a tented camp at Geneifa on the Suez Canal. Force 'Z' then became Layforce of four battalions with former No 8 Commando, now 'B' Battalion, under Lieutenant-Colonel Dermot Daly. We lacked the heavy weapons and transport of an ordinary infantry battalion.

Preparations for the Rhodes operation now got under way. I remember an outline of the beach dug into the sand which was to give us an idea of our objectives. Captain Roger Courtney and Lieutenant-Commander Clogstoun Willmott of the Folboat Section carried out a daring beach reconnaissance. But then on 6 April the Germans invaded Greece and Yugoslavia and the operation was quickly called off. In the Western Desert, too, the tide was turning the Germans' way. General Rommel, who had arrived in the desert in February, launched a surprise attack at the end of March, driving back the Western Desert Force, which had been seriously depleted by the need to send troops to Greece. By 13 April he had re-occupied Cyrenaica and encircled Tobruk. As a result of this the role of Layforce was radically changed. Some abortive raids were carried out on the Western Desert coastline, while 'B' Battalion remained at Mersa Matruh as Layforce Reserve.

On 20 May, 1941, the Germans made an airborne attack on Crete. After heavy fighting they captured Maleme airfield and rapidly brought in reinforcements. The garrison, under General Freyberg, was caught by surprise. Within a few days the German force had grown to 22,000 men. The only way the attack could be defeated was with the recapture of Maleme and GHQ Middle East saw this as an ideal task for Layforce. This it was unable to do for various reasons. The two battalions involved were not organized or trained to fight a first-class enemy in the fearsome Cretan mountains. They had no dive bombers or heavy weapons like mortars and machine guns, which the Germans had in abundance. Robert Laycock himself and a few officers and men managed to be evacuated, but for the rest, after an heroic fight, inevitably bleak surrender. This was a sad day for the war in the Mediterranean and for Layforce.

Since March, 1941, General de Gaulle had been agitating for the British to invade Vichy French Syria. But General Wavell, engaged with campaigns in North Africa, Abyssinia and Greece, managed initially to dissuade Churchill. However, on 1 May, 1941, there was a pro-fascist revolt in Iraq led by Rashid Ali, and vital RAF airfields at Habbaniyah were besieged. It then became clear that Admiral Darlan, Vichy France's Foreign Minister, had promised the Germans use of facilities in Syria and Churchill began to agitate for General Wavell to occupy the territory. A week after the final evacuation from Crete the invasion began. The main thrust to Damascus and Beirut was undertaken by 7th Australian Division. However, there was a serious obstacle – the Litani River just north of Tyre running east to west along a narrow, deep, wooded gorge. Layforce 'C' Battalion's task was to land at dawn 8 June, 1941, north of the river, seize and hold bridges over it until relieved by 75 Australian Brigade. Three attacking parties landed on time, two north of the river and one, led by Major Geoffrey Keyes, south of the river. They met stiff opposition from experienced French troops, including very effective Senegalese. The battalion acquitted itself well but at great cost – 123 casualties, a quarter of its strength.

All this time, as a junior officer in 'B' Battalion (8 Commando), I had been with Michael Kealy, Michael Alexander and others in a tented camp beside the Mediterranean at Mersa Matruh, waiting anxiously for something to happen and hoping for better luck than our comrades in Layforce when the time came for us to operate ourselves. We kept fit by marching in the desert with our men, firing our weapons on the range and swimming from fantastic sandy beaches. As we had time on our hands I thought it would be useful to take the opportunity to improve my swimming. Tom Langton, Irish Guards, a Cambridge rowing blue and one of the most powerful swimmers I have ever seen, kindly obliged.

Such was the shortage of manpower that General Wavell decided that Layforce, or what was left of it, was an expensive commodity, especially as the Royal Navy, with its high losses in ships, was unwilling to co-operate in further amphibious operations for the time being. He therefore gave orders in July, 1941, that Layforce should be disbanded. Although we were for some time afraid this might happen, when the news actually came it was deeply depressing. I remember wondering what would happen next. Luckily, we did not have to wait long. Out of the blue came a GHQ request for volunteers to go to Tobruk to undertake special patrol work. Captain Michael Kealy, Devonshire Regiment, was in command, Captain Philip Dunne, RHG, second-in-command, Gordon Alston, Royal Artillery, a good Italian speaker, Intelligence Officer; Tom Langton, Jock Lewes and myself were patrol commanders. Sixty men were considered necessary for the job. I stayed at Sidi Bishr, a tented camp near Alexandria, for a few days and then sailed to Tobruk to join the others. The sea passage was a bit hazardous as the final run into Tobruk harbour had to be done at night. Trained Australian unloading parties ensured a quick turn-round, since all ships had to be back under our own fighter cover by dawn.

I sailed up in HMS *Abdiel*, a minelayer and one of the fastest ships in the fleet. In the rush of unloading, my personal kit was thrown down to eager Australians and never seen again. Arriving in what I stood up in, I found the Detachment attached to the 18th Indian Cavalry in the line in the NW Sector of Ras el Madauar next to the Mediterranean facing the Italians. The 18th Indian Cavalry, a motor battalion, had been in the line since the beginning of the siege. They had an extremely bright, resourceful and tough commander, Colonel Prentice, who looked like Gary Cooper. The officers, Viceroy Commissioned officers and men came from the Indian countryside and I quickly learned that there was nothing these remarkable people did not know about operating in the desert by day and by night. Furthermore, they were pleased to pass on their special skills to us tyros. The 18th Cavalry were dug in on the line of the Wadi Sihel, a small, steep-sided, sand-filled valley, with some stone sangars to the west from which the enemy, an Italian motor battalion 1,000 meteres away, could be observed. On the right was the deep blue Mediterranean, on the left resolute men of 9 Australian Division.

I arrived two days after the successful 'Twin Pimples' raid which shook the sleepy Italians up a bit, but provided no much-needed prisoners. When I got out of the bumpy truck after a strange moonlit journey from the noisy harbour there was a message from Mike Kealey awaiting me: 'Welcome to Tobruk. Let us meet at nine; I have some work for you.' The random crump of bursting shells during the night did not disturb my sleep much: I was bone tired after a long journey.

Mike Kealy, with great military authority behind his soft-spoken manner, was waiting in his spartan-looking tent with Jock Lewes. He said, 'David, I would like Jock and you to prepare a plan to take some Italians as prisoners, which we failed to do on the Twin Pimples raid.' It was then I got to know and much admire Jock Lewes. He had the easy, powerful, long-ranging stride of an Australian grazier. He was born in Australia in 1915. He rowed in the Oxford boat against Tom Langton in the Cambridge one in the 1939 Race. Immediately I noticed how supremely intelligent he was, a rare conceptual thinker, a highly geared intellectual brain with practical application for everyday operational needs, and fearless too – a formidable man. We began to plan the prisoner snatch in which Jock took the lead and I, the younger and far less experienced operator, followed. I remember him giving out his orders in a clear, confident voice, with Mike Kealy, the three men to give covering fire and help get the prisoners back and myself listening. 'We will start at midnight. We will move silently and directly to the enemy positions we already know. David Sutherland and I will carry pistols, the rest sub-machine guns. I will go down the first dugout and search for and grab a prisoner. If there is no enemy there I will come out and go into the next dugout and so on till we have a prisoner.'

It was a still, warm night, a quarter moon behind clouds. Wearing khaki drill trousers, khaki shirt, rubber-soled boots and operational belt, we blended into the sand and were difficult to see. I followed 10 metres behind Jock with covering men just visible on each side. Every 200 metres we stopped, lay down and listened for three or four minutes. If it was quiet we then got up and continued. Visual signals from Jock controlled our movements. After some forty-five minutes Jock whispered to me, 'We are now deep in the enemy position. I am going down to get a prisoner. Keep an eye out for me.' We lay on the ground and watched. After a couple of minutes he emerged saying, 'Hell, there's no one there.' At this point I saw, about 30 metres away, an Italian soldier walking around. Jock saw him too, raced across and grabbed him. This unfortunate man had diarrhoea, was on his way to the lavatory and was literally caught with his trousers down; such are the bizarre fortunes of war! He was marched rapidly back to our lines where a valuable, smelly prisoner was handed over! I looked at my watch. It was 1.15 am. Not a shot had been fired.

My own feelings at being besieged in Tobruk were depression and unease. The experienced enemy had the initiative. One did not know what was going to happen next. Our job was to rest by day and patrol in no-man's-land during the night. The day, often after a spectacularly beautiful dawn, usually began with the first of four or five dive-bomber – Stuka – attacks of the day on Tobruk harbour, 12 kilometres away. There were several Bofors light anti-aircraft guns in the area firing non-stop to add to the crunch of exploding bombs. Every now and then a Stuka was hit and began to lose height. Everyone cheered. At around 4 pm each day enemy shelling began, providing a lethal mix of shrapnel and flying stones. This went on for about an hour. At first this was a bit unnerving, but soon one got to know what was coming and when, and relied on one's own robust stone sangar for protection. I lived in one of these just on the reverse slope of the Wadi Pescara, sleeping on my bedding roll with my steel helmet handy.

In order to vary the task and get some patrolling experience, I went out sometimes by day to have a close look at the Italian positions near the Mediterranean. A handsome Havildar with highly pressed khaki shirt and shorts and a moustache like Salvador Dali was my kind mentor. He showed me how to use folds in the ground to advantage. I overdid this and we came under fire from a machine gun. 'Run, Sahib,' he said as we dashed for cover. He calmly pointed out my obvious mistake. I never did this again.

The Detachment's task was to dominate no-man's-land. As the Italian motor battalion never left their positions after dark, this was not difficult to achieve. Life was monotonous but reasonably comfortable. We ate as well as could be expected and some of the best curries I have ever had were prepared by 18th Indian Cavalry. The distilled sea water was unpalatable if taken neat, and lack of fresh meat and vegetables induced desert sores which did not heal. Ascorbic acid tablets helped a bit, but that, flies and the strain of being encompassed by the enemy began to get us down.

The indomitable Admiral Sir Walter Cowan was there to cheer us up. 18th Indian Cavalry built him a personal sangar on a small ridge from which he could see what was going on. I remember returning from a boring night patrol. There in the green dawn light in his sangar, steel helmet in place, stood the little Admiral. I always stopped for a welcome chat. 'Ridden to orders again, David, I hear,' he would say. 'Found the last couple of furlongs uphill a bit sticky, Admiral!' I would reply. Astonishingly fit and hard, the Admiral hunted for many years with, I believe, the Warwickshire. I remember him saying he kept himself warm by putting a copy of *The Times* under his breeches. The Admiral was captured during the break-out from Tobruk, having fired all his revolver ammunition at a tank. He was quickly repatriated. After the war he was appointed Colonel of the 18th Indian Cavalry. This appointment gave the admirable sailor more pride and pleasure than anything else in his long and distinguished career.

Around the middle of August we moved about 12 kilometres south-west to the area around Pilastrino and occupied sangars and holes in the ground about 3 kilometres west of the fort. This was the toughest sector of the perimeter as the enemy had pushed in a substantial salient at this point in the shape of an active German Motor Battalion. Our positions on each side were held by the redoubtable Australians. Patrolling round there wasn't much fun as practically every bit of ground was covered by enemy Spandaus on fixed lines. We used to go out and back through the Australians and work our way west, sometimes listening, sometimes laying tape or lifting mines. It was a strain, as there was something on every night. I remember getting into a weapon pit with two angry black scorpions at the bottom. Never have I moved so fast to get out! At the end of August we moved and patrolled north of the salient. Here we lived in disused cisterns and each night had to patrol west along the Ras el Sihel Ridge. Shelling was nominally harassing, but air blasts in the Pilastrino Sector kept us below ground. This continued till mid-September when Mike Kealy, who was an expert in putting our point of view to senior officers, adeptly convinced General Morshead, the Australian Divison and Fortress Commander, that we were required elsewhere.

In spite of the difficult circumstances, morale was high and, since everyone was exposed to the same dangers, a spirit of comradeship grew up among the defenders. The Australians upheld their fine reputation. Tough and adaptable, they hung on doggedly when others might have wavered. This was a battle honour for them, and this Division, fighting later in the Pacific, wore the 'T' of Tobruk as its sign. The Detachment achieved much during the seven weeks on the perimeter, Jock Lewes being far and away the most daring of us all. It was unpleasant at times, but we learned by our mistakes, which is the best way.

I remember Tobruk by two different distinctive, evocative smells – warm, hospitable wafts of curry and ugly, acrid blasts of cordite!

★　　★　　★

In the war the Indian Army volunteered in their millions to fight the Germans and Japanese with us. In the Western Desert there were two first-class Indian Divisions in 8th Army. As it was, the battle for Egypt was touch and go. Without the Indian Army contribution, the battle for Egypt would have been lost early on. The same applies to Burma and the Japanese invasion of India. One can say that the Indian Army involvement in the war changed the course of world history.

5

The Rommel Raid

November, 1941

The Rommel Raid was one of the great Commando disasters of the war, but first I must explain how I came to be involved in this deadly operation. After Tobruk the remnants of 8 Commando were posted to the Commando Base Depot at Geniefa in the Canal Zone. At that time this establishment housed an increasing number of the Special Force units that had been used in East Africa, as well as the last of Layforce. Another unit that moved to Geniefa was 'C' Battalion of Layforce, No 11 Commando, which had had heavy casualties in June, forcing the Litani River crossing against Vichy French. 'C' Battalion was commanded by Lieutenant-Colonel Geoffrey Keyes (who took over when Lieutenant-Colonel Dick Pedder was killed). As it happened, Geoffrey Keyes and I were at the same house at Eton. He was about three years my senior. Before leaving for Tobruk we used to sit around comfortably in the Cecil Hotel on the Corniche in Alexandria and wait for news. One evening the Reuters tape machine started and, putting my whisky and soda aside, I went over to look. It was the list of immediate awards for the Litani River crossing and Geoffrey Keyes, with a Military Cross, came top.

To fill in time in Geniefa I took a demolition course and, with this expertise under my belt, proposed to Geoffrey Keyes that I would instruct his officers and men in demolitions in exchange for a place on the operation which we had learned was then being planned, to land deep behind German lines in the Western Desert. I had fun training them.

By October, 1941, General Auchinleck, now the Commander-in-Chief, was, under continuous pressure from Churchill, drawing up plans for a counter-offensive designed to relieve Tobruk and drive Rommel out of Cyrenaica. To support this operation, code-named 'Crusader', the Middle East Commando was given two tasks. The newly-formed 'L' Detachment Special Air Service Regiment was to raid airfields in the Gazala-Timimi area, while No 11 Commando was to penetrate further to the west. The target was a number of headquarters installations in the Cyrene area. Specifically these were Rommel's house and the German HQ, believed to be at Beda Litoria, the Italian HQ at Cyrene and the Italian Intelligence Centre at Apollonia. In addition they were to sabotage telephone and telegraph communications in the area. The attacks were to be carried out on the night 17/18 November, the eve of the launching of Crusader. Although the actual raid was under Keyes' command, Laycock was responsible for overall supervision of the operation. His plan was to divide his forces into four detachments, one for each of the objectives. They would be transported in the submarines *Torbay* and *Talisman* to a suitable point on the coast and landed by rubber boats three nights before Crusader was due to start. They would be met on the beach by John Haseldon, an Arabist, with local guides. They would then move by night, lying up by day, make a daylight reconnaissance on the 17th and attack that night. The submarines would be waiting to collect them from the fourth to the sixth nights after landing.

A force of fifty-six left Alexandria on the evening of 10 November, twenty-eight in each submarine. It was like Dante's Inferno; we were unbelievably crowded and hot, bodies lying everywhere. I was on *Talisman* and we took four days to arrive off the beach. My target was the Italian

Intelligence Centre at Apollonia, about which few details seemed to exist. I remember looking at the beach through the periscope. It was deserted, with rising hills behind. The landing went badly. *Torbay* ran in first and, getting into the sheltered side of the bay, managed to get her party of Commandos, including Keyes, ashore without incident. The weather was rough. Almost all the inflatable boats foundered in the surf and men arrived on the beach soaked to the skin. Wearing Arab dress, John Haseldon was waiting on the beach. He lit a large fire there from driftwood which was visible for miles, but essential to warm everyone up. It was a bitterly cold night.

Talisman then closed the beach to land us. The method of getting ashore was by two-man inflatable dinghy. Under each dinghy was a sealed four-gallon petrol can filled with rations and explosives. As it was cold, everyone wore warm clothes under their battledress and carried full equipment. The fourteen two-man inflatables were lined up along the forecasing from the gun-tower to the foc's'le, the idea being that the ship would submerge slowly, allowing the boats to float off. Events did not work out like that. In the inflatable next to me was Robert Laycock. We were chatting about the stars which were particularly brilliant that night. He wore the badges of a full colonel and I congratulated him on his promotion. We were just talking about the Pole Star and its importance in navigation when *Talisman* ran aground on the beach. A green sea swept over the forecasing from behind us and I saw Robert Laycock's jaw tighten as he and his companion were hurled headlong into the boiling water. Luckily I had both arms over the steel jumper wire that runs along the forecasing. I remember Sergeant Willy Moss, my team-mate, looking at me in horror as our inflatable was lifted up and then slammed back on the deck. I looked round and there were, including ours, five inflatables left. *Talisman* then went hard astern and tried to launch these inflatables. This was virtually impossible, as a strong offshore wind sprang up and as soon as an inflatable was launched from the submarine it was swept out to sea. Eventually I found myself spending some time in the sea, reaching those inflatables and getting them back to the submarine. As it was then getting late, Michael Wilmott, the Captain, decided to abandon any further attempt at landing and try again the next night. The following night the weather had deteriorated further and the landing had to be abandoned completely. *Talisman* then returned to Alexandria with myself, Willy Moss and eight others on board. It was just as well I missed the landing. Robert Laycock, Sergeant Terry and Corporal Brittlebank were the only survivors. All three hid in caves and fissures in the rocks for several weeks until the advancing 8th Army appeared on the scene.

None of the operational objectives was achieved. The losses were horrendous; of the fifty-six good men who started out, forty-three were killed, wounded or taken prisoner. Notably, Geoffrey Keyes got a posthumous VC and Robin Campbell, German interpreter, shot in the leg, a DSO. Lieutenant Roy Cook took my target, was taken prisoner and spent the rest of the war a PoW in Italy.

Why did it all go so horribly wrong? The concept of the operation was far too ambitious. There was no up-to-date target intelligence. Rommel did not use the house Keyes attacked and was in Rome on his birthday.

The landing was noticed immediately by the enemy, who reacted swiftly. To land a large Commando force on an exposed Mediterranean beach in harsh mid-November weather was far too risky.

6

With the SAS in the Western Desert

March, 1942

When the admirable Willy Moss and I arrived back in Alexandria on *Talisman* after our lucky and frightening experience people said, 'Where have you been? Why do both of you look so pale?' We replied, 'We have been working in the Egyptian salt-mines!'

There was a message from Michael Kealy for us to rejoin our unit, 1 Special Boat Section, at its base at Kabrit on the Great Bitter Lake. At that time SBS consisted of fifteen officers and forty-five other ranks. Its role was changed from enemy-held beach reconnaissance and shore-side sabotage to small-scale assault raiding. This followed the battle won by David Stirling that all raiding forces in the Middle East should come under his, 1 Special Air Service's, command. This made sense to me as I thought SBS's role was too narrow. However, there was a sharp increase in SBS casualties later on.

Life at Kabrit, the SAS/SBS training base, was all go, interest, excitement, innovation and looking forward to the next operation. The instructors were experts in putting over the various new subjects in an amusing way. Bill Cumper, a great Cockney wit: 'If you want to know anything about explosives, don't come anywhere near me!' Peter Warr gave us some excruciatingly painful parachute training when we had to jump on to the sand from a 12-foot tower aboard a moving truck. This was followed by six jumps from an RAF

Hudson to qualify as a parachutist. Like many, I disliked parachuting, an unnatural way of going into battle. For me it was purely a question of mind over matter. There were long day and night marches in the desert with heavy loads of explosives, ammunition, food and little water, so we could reach targets and fend for ourselves. There were many day and night exercises, using prismatic compass and map. Willy Moss and I often paddled across the Bitter Lake and back in a folboat with our rifles and haversacks safely stowed. Kabrit Camp was full of interesting characters.

The first SAS operation at Timimi had been a parachuting disaster due to unexpectedly high wind. I remember David Stirling limping on crutches with a damaged back. He asked about the Rommel raid. I told him it was a failure due to bad weather. I commiserated on his back injury. He replied, 'We will not risk parachuting in the desert again. I will ask the splendid Long Range Desert Group (LRDG) to deliver us to our target next time by truck.' This is what happened. Quietly taking in what was going on was a distinguished-looking figure wearing a Cameron tartan kilt and regimental tam-o'-shanter, leaning on a long stick. He came up to me and said, 'I'm Fitzroy Maclean. I am godmother to the French SAS. Who are you?' I replied, 'I am David Sutherland in the Black Watch, one of the Special Boat Section people.' Thus a rich and special friendship, later extended to his wife Veronica, began which lasted until his death. Typical of Fitzroy to use the word 'godmother' when anyone else would say 'liaison officer'. It was clever of David Stirling to find Fitzroy, with his fluent French and diplomatic background, unique qualifications for introducing to the SAS the remarkable French officers, Bergé, Jordan and others, who had joined General de Gaulle, and keeping an experienced eye on their initiation.

One larger-than-life character in the SAS at Kabrit in those days was Paddy Mayne. Well over 6 foot, an Irish Rugby International and heavyweight boxer with red hair and blue eyes, he was a Captain in the Royal Ulster Rifles. It is said that he hit his commanding officer when the latter's conduct at the Litani River crossing displeased him. He ended up in detention, from which he was rescued by David Stirling. I can well believe this as Paddy had a notoriously short temper. If he didn't like you, you had better watch out. I remember an evening at the officers' mess bar going out for a pee and returning to find a body on the floor and Paddy rubbing his right fist. 'Oh, he bored me!' was Paddy's laconic comment. Behind this fearsome exterior lay a brilliant operational brain. In camp he had a tent set apart in which his formidable bulk lay on a number of rubber parachute training mattresses piled high like a Pasha. I remember the day he was awarded his first DSO (of four) for an incredible feat of German plane destruction in the desert. Like a young Boy Scout, I slipped quietly into the presence to congratulate him. 'Thank you very much, just below the VC they tell me.' 'We don't want you to be killed,' I ventured reassuringly. 'Don't worry – that won't happen,' and he turned over and went to sleep! Luckily for us and unluckily for the Germans, miraculously he survived the war.

Alas, the same cannot be said for Jock Lewes. Immediately after Tobruk Jock was picked by David Stirling to join him, Paddy Mayne and Bill Fraser to get the SAS started as a new, effective and professional unit. They, together with the NCOs Pat Riley, Jim Almonds, Bob Bennett and others, are known as 'The Originals'. Jock quickly saw the need for a reliable, easy-to-make and easy-to-place explosive charge for use against enemy planes and other targets. After experimenting, he came up with the formula plastic high explosive, thermite and diesel oil. This lethal mixture could be worked safely on a table like dough, put into a cotton bag with an explosive primer and detonating cord to which was added a simple time-delay fuse, and you have the 'Lewes bomb'. This safe-to-use, versatile, very powerful bomb accounted for hundreds of enemy aircraft and many other targets like bomb and petrol dumps at the hands of the SAS during the war. It was used by the SAS in the Falklands War to destroy Argentine planes on Pebble Island. And so the name of the remarkable Jock Lewes lives on. I believe he designed the SAS Regimental Badge and motto. The dark blue element in the SAS Regimental Colours derives from Jock being an Oxford rowing blue.

To reinforce the success of earlier raids, in December, 1941, David Stirling decided to attack airfields in the Gulf of Sirte for the second time. Paddy Mayne took Tamet, Stirling Sirte and Jock Lewes Nofilia. This was an area 400 miles beyond the Egyptian frontier deep behind enemy lines. Mayne destroyed twenty-seven aircraft. Stirling found Sirte airfield alert and destroyed twelve supply trucks outside. Lewes found two aircraft on Nofilia which were destroyed. The enemy was wide awake. When his group were on their way to the rendezvous with the LRDG they were spotted by a low-flying Savoia which circled round firing at them. The plane then made another run. This time Lewes was hit and died almost at once. It was 30 December, 1941. He was twenty-six. Thus an SAS 'meteor' disappeared.

Cairo is an Eastern Muslim city; Alexandria, since it was founded by a Greek, a Western European one. For me, both cities were important during the war for a most welcome and much-needed change of scene and pace. I began to appreciate good food as well! Each city had its own special atmosphere. Because there was much traffic on the hot, sandy road, one allowed over two hours to drive from the comfortable peace and order of Kabrit Camp to the ugly hurly-burly of Cairo, the last ten miles through one of the great slums of Africa. Ancient, groaning camels heavily laden with sacks of grain and large panniers of wood, and diminutive donkeys struggling with huge loads of hay and alfalfa mingled with the masses of the people wearing the jallabiya and turban. Usually our destination was Shepheard's Hotel. The famous terrace set about with wicker chairs and tables provided a lofty and shaded view of Ibrahim Pasha Street. Inside was the Moorish Hall, delightfully cool and lit by a dome of coloured glass. There were small groups sitting comfortably in plump armchairs around small octagonal tables. It gave a feeling of intimacy and discretion. From the Moorish Hall the great staircase swept upwards to the well-appointed bedrooms. The food was in plentiful supply, and good. Presiding over the men-only long bar was Joe, the Swiss barman, probably one of the best-informed people in Cairo. Perhaps he knew more about the next SAS operation than I did, perhaps he didn't! His anti-hangover potion, 'Suffering Bastard', the ingredients of which he would never reveal, was magically effective.

As Cairo housed the Commander and Staff of GHQ Middle East, the city was full of officers and men in uniform. The Sporting Club on Gezira Island was a good place to eat and relax. There one could enjoy a large cold table followed by a sleep for a couple of hours and swim in the magnificent pool, all without spending much money. I remember Cairo as velvet cool and bracing in the winter, but oven-like and stuffy in June, July and August, when everyone moved to Alexandria to be near the sea.

Alexandria was the HQ and base of both the Mediterranean Fleet and the submarine flotilla. At that time the Germans and Italians had complete air superiority over the Eastern Mediterranean. The only way SBS could reach its targets and back was by Greek and HM submarine. Taking SBS to and from their raiding party tasks had to be fitted into a big submarine patrol programme. We began to train with the splendid Greek and British submarine crews in Alexandria Harbour on their rare days off.

For me personally, and for many of my friends, wartime Alexandria life-style was immensely exhanced by the 'Quartier Grec'. In those days Greek families such as the Benachis, Rodocanachis, Casullis, Stathatos and others ran Alexandria.

They were all hospitable, intelligent and fun to be with. Just as events for the Allies nosedived before the Battle of Alamein in October, 1942, so the Greeks became more supportive. In Alexandria I stayed in the Cecil Hotel on the Corniche, where the Manager was a competent British Jew, Mr Metzger. It offered good food and a barber who rubbed one's face with a block of ice after a shave. There were plenty of fine restaurants: the Union Bar for grilled quail on a bed of rice with a cognac sauce, and the Alexandria Sporting Club, with racing, wining, dining, swimming and dancing in place.

On 1 March, 1942, Willy Moss and I received a message to return to Kabrit for an SAS operation in the Western Desert. The jeep journey from Alexandria took six hours – three to Cairo and three on. We wondered what kind of operation lay ahead. Next day there was a briefing in the SAS operations room at 9 am. Pinned to a large board were maps of the Western Desert and the city of Benghazi and its approaches. Looking closely at the maps were David Stirling, Paddy Mayne, Bob Melot, an Arabist, Gordon Alston, Italian speaker, and Captain Allott, SBS. I joined them. Giving out orders, David Stirling stood up and spoke in a quiet, confident manner, with no trace of his recent back injury. Stirling began by saying that he now wanted to change the direction of SAS attacks. Hitherto German aircraft had been the profitable target. However, as the Desert War was a battle of supplies, he intended to attack shipping in Benghazi Harbour. Two canoes and limpet mines were required. As no one had ever made the 400-mile journey to Benghazi before, there was discussion on how we should best get into and out of Benghazi undetected. Starting from the LRDG base at Siwa Oasis, we decided to use a Ford truck disguised to look like a German staff car carrying Stirling, Mayne and Melot, and an actual German staff car which had been captured driven by me, with Alston beside me and Moss in the back. Mayne was dozing in a large armchair while Stirling was talking, perhaps implying that enemy planes were more important targets than ships.

We drove down the sandy desert road from Mersa Matruh south to Siwa, a magical spring morning with cirrus clouds high in the sky. After some three hours a thin line of date palms appeared on the horizon. The oasis was about 10 kilometres in diameter, and soon we saw masses of dates piled into heaps – dates being the sole trade. Siwa had a strange, timeless, Biblical feeling about it, as if the ancient oracle was still there. We drove to the centre to see an imposing-looking mosque and a warren of hovels built of mud. This was the fortress town of the Senussi. Unwisely, the Italians, over the years, had given the Senussi a hard time, so they were pleased to work for us and with us as guides and providers of intelligence about the enemy. There was time in Siwa to have refreshing swims in the sulphur pools. It was like bathing in azure blue soda-water.

As we were waiting to leave for Benghazi, I met a tall, good-looking man, his face burnt by the desert sun. It was John Olivey, Commander of the LRDG Rhodesian Patrol. 'Welcome to Siwa,' he said. He took me to meet some of his NCOs and men. Under a clearing in the palm trees an impressive bunch of men were cleaning weapons and loading camouflage nets, jerricans of petrol, water, ammunition, crates of food, our canoes, and their personal bedding roll, etc, on to desert-worthy three-ton trucks. 'Good to have you with us. You're joining the best patrol in the business. To and from Benghazi will be like a Cook's Tour. You wait!' A stream of thoughts and feelings were leaping in on me. I was alive with the excitement of being with Stirling and Mayne on such an early operation. 'L' Detachment SAS was only four months old. How would I react to events under their stern gaze?

After a good night's sleep we left Siwa at 10 am on 15 March, 1942. There was a wind from the west in our faces.

The German staff car was compact and easy to drive, being independently sprung. It had left-hand drive and Gordon Alston was sitting on my right with Willy Moss behind me. There were ten vehicles in the group: Olivey, followed by his navigator, next the disguised Ford staff car, then the real German staff car, and, bringing up the rear, the six heavily laden three-ton trucks.

We followed a well-worn track north-west from Siwa and after about 30 miles went through a large gap in the Egyptian frontier wire. I said to myself and to Alson, 'So far, so good.' He smiled. In the afternoon we stopped, changed drivers and added petrol. There was little leg-room in the back, so Moss got out for a walk. We were heading west and wore sun goggles.

Before dusk we stopped for the night. Cooking fires were quickly lit, using a mixture of petrol and sand. In no time a splendid meal of hot soup, meat and vegetables (M and V), fruit salad and tea laced with rum appeared. We discussed the day's drive as we sat round a fire and listened to the news from the BBC. There were reports of bombing in London. While this was going on, the navigator with theodolite and sextant was plotting our exact position in the desert. The night sky was cold, clear and bright with stars. When I had settled my hip into the soft sand I slept well. Next day was uneventful. Alston and I took turns to drive. He was a more natural, experienced driver than me, having worked with an Italian motor-racing team in Italy before the war. The desert scene became more varied with dips and gullies and attractive spring flowers. Around the camp fire that night, Stirling, Mayne, Alston, Allott and I were bemoaning Jock Lewes's untimely death.

Next day we continued on the old Caravan Route, the Trigh el Abd, the route of the slaves. This road had been used by both sides in various desert advances and was extensively mined. I remember driving along happily chatting to Alston about the fun he must have had in Italy before the war when I saw to my left and slightly below some flowers and scrappy bushes which I decided to drive through. This proved to be a great mistake! Ahead, but too late to avoid, I saw an Italian thermos bomb lying in the scrub. These effective mines were dropped from aircraft and armed by mercury switch. There was a sudden devastating explosion and the left front wheel blew off and vanished. The car buckled crazily and turned on its side. There was an eerie silence as the engine stopped. I remember Alston miraculously standing up as if nothing had happened and Moss quietly looking at my left arm. It was a minute or two before I could hear properly and regain my balance. Meanwhile the Ford staff car with Stirling, Mayne, Melot and John Olivey drove over to see what had happened. I had virtually no pain, but an ugly chunk had been taken out of my left wrist and some small pieces of metal from the staff car driven into my left arm. They all discussed what should be done. Stirling, with a worried expression, came over and said reassuringly, 'David, I know you want to go on but your wound is too bad for that. We are sending you back to Siwa now on a three-tonner. This is bad luck but there it is.'

The patrol stopped for about an hour so the vehicle load could be moved around and all the unwanted stuff go back to Siwa with me. Alston and Moss moved on with the others. They were impatient to make up lost time and I wished them luck as they headed west. The three-ton driver was one of the best in the LRDG and knew the desert well. It must have been boring for him to leave an interesting operation and return to base alone with me. He was kind, considerate and helpful to a tee, and kept an eye on the large shell dressing I had on my damaged wrist. By following our earlier tracks in two-and-a-half days I was back in Siwa. As it happened, the operation in Benghazi Harbour was called off because of bad weather and a damaged canoe. Mayne destroyed fifteen aircraft at Berka airfield. So I did not miss much. At Siwa I saw the efficient LRDG doctor, who packed my wrist with penicillin and sent me to 8th General Hospital in Alexandria via Mersa Matruh.

One morning I woke up in the Alexandria Hospital to find an attractive girl sitting near me. Let me explain. When the Layforce officers hit Alexandria in the summer of 1941 three pretty, bright, Greek girls appeared: Ivy Vassilopoulo, fair, athletic, like the goddess Atalanta; Jenny Dimopoulo, dark, hair like Carmen; Teresa (Thessy) Whitfield, brunette, with spectacular dress sense and model figure. They were known to the Layforce officers as 'The Three Graces'.

Thessy and I met at an Officers' Club dance and got on well. She was sophisticated, spoke four languages and was fun to be with. Whenever I was in Alexandria staying at the Cecil Hotel I would give her a ring and arrange to meet. We talked about life in Alexandria, her many friends, and how the war was going, usually badly for us. We had delicious meals at seafood restaurants, Pastrudi's or the Union Bar, and swam and danced at the Alexandria Sporting Club. She had a natural way of dressing. When she pinned up her hair the effect was stunning. In a short while I left hospital. Thessy's family had a beach hut at Sidi Bishr, ideal for sun and swimming. I made a rapid recovery.

7

The Aluite Plan

April–May, 1942

In April, 1942, Rommel was driving eastwards towards the Nile while Kleist's Army Group South threatened the Caucasus. If both broke through it seemed probable to strategists in Whitehall and Cairo that they might aim for a link-up at the head of the Persian Gulf, towards which Kleist's forces must pass through Syria, in which case Special Service troops left behind might fight as guerrillas, and knowledge of beaches across which they might be reinforced and supplied would be of value.

There was only one unit in the Middle East theatre with the required beach reconnaissance skills – the SBS. On 15 April SBS was ordered to carry out a detailed reconnaissance of every beach suitable for Special Service troops landing between the Palestine/Lebanon border in the south and the Syria-Turkey border in the north. Some twenty beaches were involved and six weeks allotted for the task. I was sitting around at Kabrit when Tom Montgomery, a Captain in the Black Watch who had recently joined the SBS, sent for me. 'We have an important beach reconnaissance job to do at once.' He described the task. 'You and others will be needed in the team.' I drove up to Beirut in a jeep and trailer with Michael Alexander and we pulled off the road for the night in an orange grove on the southern outskirts of Haifa. Tom Langton and Eric Newby followed us the next day. As coordinator, Montgomery rented, as a base, a large house in the beautiful hills above Beirut at Bic Fayar. This was top secret, detailed beach reconnaissance work which had to be done right and in a hurry. Montgomery divided the beaches: Syria for Langton and Newby; Lebanon to Alexander and me. So for all of us and the admirable Sergeant Sherwood a time of welcome change of scene and pace appeared. As there was no limit on expenses, we lived well in the best beach-side hotels and inns. It was hard work, up at dawn sketching and photographing each beach in question. We had help from the Royal Navy, who provided two shallow-draft 'R' boats for taking beach soundings. Each evening we wrote up our reports before collapsing into bed.

I remember driving in a jeep into the wooded hills about 10 miles from the sea with an army officer whose job it was to fix on the map the exact spot of the arms dumps left for guerrilla forces to use. He had no problem with most. However, one site he found a problem, and asked for my help. The dump, deep in the forest, had been well camouflaged with fabric painted to look like a pile of stones. Below it were three steep ravines. It took me about half an hour, using binoculars, compass and map, to fix exactly where the dump was. I marked the spot on my companion's map. I wondered how the dump fabric would stand up to the winter rains.

On Saturdays we drove to Bic Fayar to hand in the week's reports; they were then re-drawn by Royal Engineers. Sunday was spent having a good time in Beirut, usually at the St George's Hotel. We finished the work two days before the deadline. For me it was a fascinating introduction to the Levant – the outlines of the ancient Crusader castles, Krak des Chevaliers and Markab, against a lovely sky, the smell of Arab coffee and orange blossom, the sweet honey taste of baklava.

Though the positions at Alamein and Stalingrad were to hold and the threat never became real, the work carried out by the SBS, the Aluite Plan, named after the Syrian tribe, gave us experience of operational survey and reconnaissance.

Also it enabled us to get to know and like the tough, observant and extremely funny Eric Newby. His tales of life in the fo'c's'le of *Moshulu* on the Last Grain Race were hilarious.

After six weeks of excellent food, wine, sun and sea air my left wrist was as good as new.

8

Attacking German Airfields in Crete

June, 1942

During the war the island of Crete was important to the Germans, not because of its land which is mountainous, but because of its airfields. Turn the map of Greece and the Eastern Mediterranean upside down and look at it from the enemy point of view. Aircraft based on Crete were well placed to attack shipping and dominate the sea lanes in the Eastern End of the Mediterranean. Also, these airfields provided useful staging points for reinforcing Rommel's Desert Army by air. There were four operational airfields of interest to raiding force planners in Cairo and to us, the SBS – Maleme in the west, Heraklion in the east, Kastelli in the centre and Tymbaki in the south.

The island of Malta was rapidly approaching starvation. An important convoy was scheduled to leave Alexandria for Malta on 11 June, 1942. The attack on Cretan airfields was specifically in support of this convoy. The plan was to attack all four airfields on Crete simultaneously at midnight on the night of 12 June. The SBS was given this mission, while the task of attacking four airfields in Libya fell to the SAS. On 30 May, having completed the Aluite Plan, I was back at the SBS base at Kabrit. Michael Kealy arrived hot-foot and furious from Cairo. He wanted to give us orders, with a large map of Crete on the wall behind him. He began to speak in his gentle, precise way. Listening and taking notes were

James Allott, George Duncan of the Black Watch in his special khaki knee-breeches, and myself.

Maleme was the largest, most heavily defended airfield, and from our point of view the most difficult to get at. Kealy and Allott took this target for themselves. Duncan was directed to Kastelli, myself to Tymbaki. There was no mention of Heraklion airfield, which I thought was a bit odd, but I let this pass. It was exciting to be back in action with trusted friends so soon after the desert thermos bomb disaster and given an airfield target to attack myself. After some hurried training, the Maleme group left Alexandria in the evening of 6 June aboard the Greek submarine *Papanikolis*. After a long, difficult march, Kealy and Allott decided that Maleme airfield was too well guarded to give them the slightest chance of success. The Germans had lost many thousands of their crack troops in the fight for Maleme the year before and had no intention of surrendering it or allowing infiltration. It was completely surrounded by wire fences, at least one of which was electrified. Machine-gun posts and searchlights had been installed at tactically well chosen points around it. There were so many guard dogs about that, according to Allott, 'It sounded like Cruft's on show day!' From then on we did not consider Maleme airfield a suitable SBS target – it was too dangerous.

The Kastelli and Tymbaki groups were to sail from Bardia to Crete on the 10-ton motor-boat *Porcupine*, commanded by John Campbell, one of the great SOE skippers of the war. As space on the boat was tight and room had to be made on the return trip to Egypt for Cretans fleeing for their lives, we cut the SBS group to six: Duncan, Barnes and McKenzie to Kastelli; Moss, Brittlebank and myself to Tymbaki. Brittlebank was an interesting character. A corporal in the Royal Artillery, he was known in the SBS as 'the Bombardier'. He first came to favourable notice during an appallingly difficult and testing exercise for Layforce on the island of Arran in the winter of 1940. Almost bald, he had the strength and mental agility of a scrum half. He was one of the three survivors from the ill-fated Rommel Raid. He kept alive by chewing roots and leaves with occasional bread from friendly Senussi. He gave a hilarious account of these 'desert experiences' when he finally turned up at Kabrit. I discussed with Willy Moss who the third member of the Tymbaki team should be. We both went for 'the Bombardier'.

Bardia was well known for its wells of pure, clear water. In the afternoon of 6 June we arrived there in a couple of heavily laden trucks from our advanced base at Mersa Matruh. For the last hour we drove slap into the setting sun. It was airless, ovenlike. There was a lot of traffic on the road, against us, heading east. Looking down, the shell-damaged houses and well-protected harbour of Bardia appeared below. There was a small, inoffensive-looking motor launch made fast to the harbour wall. It was *Porcupine*. There was ample road space in the harbour for our truck to park. We began to unload our operational stores and equipment. While this was going on, a stocky man in his 30s, wearing the khaki drill and insignia of a naval Lieutenant-Commander and the ribbon of the DSO, introduced himself. 'I am John Campbell. Welcome to Bardia. You are coming with me to Crete and back.' His voice reminded me of the seafarers from the Western Isles. John Campbell had created a comfortable base in the low harbour buildings near to *Porcupine*. There was a memorable dinner with him presiding. The cheese soufflé and rum baba were excellent. We toasted the success of the first SBS operation on Crete. Using a comfortable bunk, I enjoyed the best night's sleep I had had for ages. I remember taking advantage of the soft Bardia water and had a good close shave the next morning. We filled our water bottles before sailing.

The distance from Bardia to the southern point of Crete is about 200 miles. We checked that all our operational equipment, Lewes bombs, weapons, ammunition, food, water, etc, was on board before *Porcupine* left Bardia at 10 am on 7 June. It was exciting to be on my fourth operation with the

SBS and to hope that, with two excellent men with me, we would have success on this important operation to protect the Malta convoy. Also, at midsummer of 1942, to redress the balance against the Germans, who were having it all their own way at that stage of the war.

Moss and the Bombardier were snoozing in the shade, legs up on a pile of kit. I said to myself, 'Sensible people'. We approached Crete at dusk. With my binoculars I could see on the far skyline the massive outline of Mount Ida. The air was full of the smell of wild thyme and asphodels. It was a moonless night. I went into the wheelhouse. John Campbell, his face illuminated by the dim compass light, said, 'We'll be landing in about half an hour.'

For the last stretch the launch crept in at low throttle. The crew communicated in whispers, as eyes strained ahead for the recognition signal. Two letters in morse. Everyone exclaimed at once in an excited whisper when it finally came. *Porcupine* stopped about 30 yards offshore. There was a slight swell. Rubber dinghies were inflated and Duncan, Barnes and McKenzie and all their operational group for Kastelli were rowed ashore in one, myself and the Tymbaki group in another. The beach, a sandy cove with submerged boulders, suddenly came alive, with many people rushing towards us out of the darkness speaking Greek. These Cretans, wearing black headcloths with tiny tassels and leather breeches, greeted everyone in sight with shouts and embraces. Suddenly the most villainous-looking one appeared and said in perfect English, 'I am Tom Dunbabin – welcome to Crete.' I helped a Cretan grandfather who could not swim into one of the inflatables. When *Porcupine* turned about with the throbbing putter from its engine, slowly disappearing, our link with the outside world was broken.

Tom Dunbabin, archaeologist and Cretan scholar, had been living and working in the Cretan mountains since the German invasion the year before. He was the senior British Liaison Officer in Crete, co-ordinating the resistance against

German occupation. He reported direct to Special Operations Executive (SOE) Headquarters in Cairo. On the morning of 8 June, sitting in a large, shady cave from which the sea was clearly visible below, Tom Dunbabin briefed us. Without notes, he started with a brilliant conceptual analysis of where the Germans had got to in their occupation of Crete. He went on to say how important, at the peak of German power, the four airfields in Crete were for reinforcing the Afrika Corps' expected advance on the Nile Delta and the significance of protecting the Malta convoy. As we did not know the country and its ways, he would provide local guides and helpers to set us quickly and safely towards our targets.

I had the special privilege of being with the SBS on Crete on three occasions during the war: this time in June, 1942; a year later before the invasion of Italy; and Christmas, 1944, in Heraklion, when Italy had surrendered and the German garrison withdrawn to the Maleme–Canea area. One always remembers most clearly one's first encounter with Crete. For me it is Tom Dunbabin's briefing *tour de force*. Sitting nearby were two fit young men with sunburnt faces and splendid-looking boots. Tom came over and said, 'Here are your guides; they know the Tymbaki area well. They are shepherds.'

At dusk in the cave we had a large hot meal of tomato soup, meat and vegetable stew, cheese, peaches and coffee, which all of us, particularly the guides, consumed with gusto. At nightfall the Kastelli Group left with two guides. I walked with Duncan, Barnes, McKenzie and their guides for half an hour on their track going north-east, before wishing them luck and turning back. They were in fine form. I had decided that, as Tymbaki airfield was so much nearer than Kastelli, we could sleep and leave next day.

The Cretan mountains are formidable. As we had two rugged ridges and valleys to get over at night, we took our time. Looking down from a cave on to Tymbaki airfield we saw buildings but no aircraft. Clearly they had been moved. This was really disappointing for all of us. We looked at each other as we ground our teeth in disgust. In those days target intelligence was rudimentary and often out of date. I felt the best thing to do was to move slowly back to the beach, which we did. The Kastelli group, however, were much more fortunate, destroying eight aircraft, six trucks and bomb and petrol dumps; they returned to the beach in high spirits and pleased with themselves.

As *Porcupine* was not due to pick us up till 23 June, we had time on our hands. I used to get up at dawn, the most interesting and exciting moment of the day, walk into the hillside and watch what was going on until the fierce summer heat drove me back into the shade. One morning, with a spectacular dawn and the rippling sea sparkling below, I saw a lone figure approaching. He was wearing khaki shorts and shirt, and had a jaunty way of walking. I held him in my binoculars and could not believe my eyes: it was George Jellicoe. I walked down to the track to meet him. He was the sole survivor of a group of four French SAS who had landed from the Greek submarine *Triton* on 10 June, paddled ashore and destroyed twenty-one German aircraft at Heraklion airfield. This hazardous and successful raid had run into trouble from the start. The large distance over rugged ground, plus the heavy loads to be carried, slowed the group. The German reaction was rapid. In a fierce fight one French soldier was killed and the other three, including the Commander, Bergé, taken prisoner. Sixty Cretans had been executed as a reprisal and the Cretan guide, Lieutenant Kosta Petrakis, forced to flee the island with his brothers and sisters.

I remember turning to George and saying, 'Why don't we get out of this fierce sun for a bit and go into that cave and you can fill me in on what happened at Heraklion?' At the cave's mouth I was almost knocked down by a couple of aged goats rapidly departing. From George's cogent account of the spectacularly successful operation I twigged why Mike Kealy was so furious at the operational briefing at Kabrit, 30 May, and why he did not mention Heraklion as an SBS target. David Stirling had intervened with the Cairo planners and Heraklion, the most juicy airfield target in Crete, given to the French SAS. At this point our welcome conversation ended in disorder. I began scratching my back like an ape and realized I was infested with goat fleas, George likewise. I took off my shirt and crushed 100 fleas nose to tail in the lining, before taking it off and laying it in the sun. Luckily help was at hand. That night John Campbell and *Porcupine* picked us up. We had a full load of escaping Cretans. On our way back from Crete the coxswain of *Porcupine* took some amusing photographs. I am deep in thought about why there were no German planes at Tymbaki. Near me was a stunning-looking Cretan girl, presumably one of Kosta Petrakis's sisters! After two days at sea we made Mersa Matruh just before it fell to the Germans. A waiting truck took us to Alexandria. It took a long time for George Jellicoe and I to get rid of the fleas!

It should be noted that although twenty-nine enemy aircraft were destroyed in Crete and twenty in the Western Desert, nevertheless fifteen out of the seventeen ships in the Malta convoy were sunk. The two ships that got through, however, saved Malta.

9

Operation Anglo

September, 1942

Some years after the war Mr Churchill was asked which period for him had been the most anxious. He answered without hesitation, 'September and October, 1942'. With hindsight one can see that these months were the turning-point of the war; soon the balance would swing in favour of the Allies. However, the great battles around Stalingrad were in their early stages, the war in the Pacific unresolved and Rommel's desert army at Alamein still with the power to drive through to the Nile and across the Sinai to the vital Gulf oilfields, there perhaps to meet triumphant German armies pouring down through the Caucasus. To prevent this and restore morale, General Alexander replaced General Auchinleck in August, 1942, and General Montgomery took command of 8th Army.

At that time the highest priority was given to eliminating enemy aircraft based on Crete and Rhodes, which were successfully attacking shipping in the Eastern Mediterranean and bombing and photographing military targets in Egypt. The only way SBS could get to the airfields and back was by submarine. This called for sophisticated operational planning.

The Luftwaffe and the Regia Aeronautica were using two operational airfields on Rhodes from which to harass Allied shipping in the Eastern Mediterranean, and also to exercise almost complete control over the seaways up and into the

Aegean. The airfields were Maritsa in the north of the island and Calatos halfway down the eastern coastline. For some months the planning staff at GHQ Middle East had kept the idea of attacking every airfield on Rhodes on the back burner. In July, 1942, it became imperative that 'something must be done'. The task was given to the SBS, was called Operation ANGLO, and a special planning team set up at GHQ under Alan Palmer of the Reading biscuit family. And so I became involved in an important raid which taxed me to the limit and from which I was lucky to return.

In the summer of 1942 there was a flap in Egypt when people thought Rommel's army might capture Cairo. There were clouds of smoke hanging over the city as secret papers were hurriedly burnt. For security reasons HQ Mediterranean Fleet moved from Alexandria to Beirut and 1st Submarine Flotilla did the same. This is why Operation ANGLO was mounted from Beirut.

When considering what to include in this book about Operation ANGLO, there are three intertwining elements: my operational report, which I have kept, a visit some years ago, as the guest of George Vroohos, to Rhodes to study the ground and meet and thank the people who had helped us, and, more recently, conversation with the admirable Commander Michael St John who commanded HM Submarine *Traveller* at the time.

It was decided that we should attack aircraft on Calatos and Maritsa airfields simultaneously at midnight on 12 September. The landing place, which we chose from an air photograph, was 500 metres east of Cape Feraclo. We hoped there would be caves and holes in the cliff where we could hide the boats for our re-embarkation, and store tins of food. To cover the 50 kilometres to Maritsa and back we allocated ten days. Intelligence on Rhodes was non-existent. The garrison was made up of 30,000 Italians. We had no wireless with which to communicate, so we were locked into a fixed timetable – landed night 4/5 September, picked up night 17/

18 September. The submarines *Papanikolis* and *Traveller* had tight patrol programmes into which SBS landings and pick-ups had to be fitted. This was one of the SBS pioneering raids with all the flaws.

On 31 August twelve SBS embarked in Beirut on RHN Submarine *Papanikolis*, Captain Allott, myself, Sergeant Moss, five men, two interpreters and two guides. We loaded our operational equipment, boats, explosives (Lewes bombs), reserve food and water on. I remember a baking, airless day. For two hours we headed north on the surface on the noisy main diesel engines. I took a last look at the Lebanon Mountains illuminated in a spectacular sunset before going below wondering how this long and difficult operation would turn out. It was excitement and anticipation for me. The Commander of *Papanikolis* was Commander Svanidis. The submarine was old. In one or two places there were leaks. With twelve extra on board and all the operational stores and equipment piled in a heap under the forward hatch, we were very crowded. It was hot and difficult to sleep. The officers and crew gave up their bunks for us and fed us well. To avoid enemy aircraft, we spent the days submerged and nights on the surface, when we could increase speed and recharge batteries. This continued for five days and nights.

Deep asleep on the afternoon of 4 September, I was woken by a Greek seaman shaking my arm with a message from the Captain: 'He wants you to look at the beach through the periscope now.' Allott was already there. I noticed his forearm muscles flex as Svanidis rotated the periscope. He turned to me with a grin and sweat on his lined forehead. 'There is your beach. Have a look!' What I saw was sensational: Mount Elias and its attendant foothills, coves and beaches etched in full afternoon sunlight. Admittedly I had been in the subarmine dark for five days, but even so the view was stunning, and to show my appreciation I gave a thumbs-up sign. It is interesting that within a short time this Arcadian scene should become for us a grim theatre of grinding fatigue, abject frustration and deadly fear.

At 2100 we surfaced and approached the shore. It was a moonless, flat calm night, bright with stars. At 2200 we got the folboat on deck and rigged it, followed by the three floats which were inflated by an air line from the submarine. Our operational equipment, food and water were loaded on to the floats. With Allott and Moss leading in the folboat, we followed in three floats. As the submarine slowly submerged to let us float clear, I heard a voice from the darkness saying, '*Kali tiki*' – 'Good luck'.

It took about two hours for us to hit the beach. We made slow progress as the inflatables were heavily loaded and difficult to paddle. Every now and then Allott and Moss in the folboat came to check we were on course. There was a slight set from the north-east. Throughout, our approach was dominated by the dark skyline of Mount Elias, which I recalled from the periscope preview. We landed about 500 metres to the west of the intended spot. I looked at my wrist-watch, a waterproof Longines with an illuminated dial I had bought in Alexandria. It was midnight. We began to take the air out of the inflatables and dismantle the folboat. Fortunately, the beach on which we landed afforded far better cover for hiding boats and food than the place intended. It was well sheltered from both sides, with some four metres of coarse sand and larger fissures and caves in the rock cliff-face directly behind. It was, in fact, an ideal landing-place for such a large raiding group. The boats were carefully hidden among the rocks, together with four days' food and four gallons of water.

Captain Allott came over and said, 'Would you and Sergeant Moss check the beach to see there is nothing left there?' The moon was rising and, looking closely, Moss and I saw some footmarks in the sand. I told Moss to get some branches from bushes growing on the cliff wall. Using these as brushes, we carefully removed the offending traces in the manner we had practised on countless exercises.

The cliff was much higher and more rugged than we had expected. We had the 'army issue' infantry pack, small haversack and operational belt with water-bottle each. The men carried .45 tommy-guns, officers .38 revolvers. We wore khaki shirts and shorts, desert boots, khaki trousers, thick sweaters for night and to keep off the mosquitoes, cap comforters on the head and camouflage nets round the neck. We wore no insignia or badges of rank. With ten days' food, water, Lewes bombs, weapons and ammunition we were seriously overloaded. It took me about thirty minutes to reach the top of the cliff, carrying around 50 lbs. Everyone was breathing hard. I saw George Tsoucas, who was some years older than the rest of us, stuck half-way. I went down, relieved him of his awkward load and helped him to the top. It was 2 am and Allott had already sent Moss and the guides to find a place in the open ground well above the cliff where we could conceal ourselves and our kit, sleep and rest the next day before moving on to our targets that night. The guides found a cave facing out to sea large enough to hold all twelve of us and our equipment. Marine Barrow was ordered to be 'on watch'. I slept fitfully and remember George Calambokidis, the interpreter, snoring to wake the dead!

We spent the next day in the cave, out of the fierce September heat, and ate bully beef and biscuits, washed down with strong, sweet tea. There was no sign of the enemy. At dusk Allott and I walked out of the cave to find the sea shining below and a vent of hot air from the sun-baked land surging past us into the sky. We moved off at 2200 with the aim of crossing the Malona-Massari road just after midnight. According to the map and the guides this could easily be accomplished if the correct route were taken. Spare equipment, Mae Wests and signalling torches were hidden in the cave in preparation for re-embarkation.

From this moment onwards the going was extremely difficult and, together with the heavy load and the doubt of the guides as to the right route to take, the progress of the party was exceptionally slow. Due to frequent halts the distance covered by 0400 was little over a mile, when Captain Allott and I decided that it was out of the question to cross the road that night. We therefore searched for a hideout and eventually found a grotto capable of accommodating the whole party. Once established there, the guides were sent to fill twelve water-bottles from a source which they said they knew of near the road. However, they returned just before dawn without water, reporting enemy activity in the neighbourhood of their destination. The next day was spent without water but in the shade. During the day I observed enemy activity in the valley between Massari and Calatos, on the aerodrome itself, and noted various positions and defence systems.

Night 6/7. Before dusk the guides were sent to recce the route for the night's march, as it was imperative to reach the road if water was to be obtained. They still insisted on keeping to the side of Mount Elias in lieu of the valley, which they believed to be patrolled after dark. A similar march to that of the night before resulted, and again the party made its final halt about one mile from the Malona bridge. Owing to the nature of the ground and the loads they were carrying, the Greek interpreters showed distinct signs of exhaustion, due to lack of training in such marching, and slowed the party down by frequent halts. Determined to get water that night, I sent the guides, together with marines Barrow and Harris, into the valley with instructions not to return without fourteen water-bottles filled. They returned just after first light and the party laid up on the hillside directly opposite Massari.

Two valuable nights had thus been wasted by taking the mountain route. The guides at first said they knew the way, but later openly confessed that they were ignorant of their surroundings. One can hardly blame them as they volunteered to come on the operation at great risk to themselves. It is, however, advisable to ascertain how much a guide really knows about the country before entrusting him to lead a party. It is better to have no guide than a bad one.

Captain Allott and I decided that, for the sake of speed on his journey to Maritsa, the parties should separate on the night 7/8. This meant that he had five nights in which to reach his objective, operate on the night of 12/13 and still have five nights clear to make his way back to the beach. I also advocated lightening the load by carrying minimum food and dumping all excess weight where we were lying up, to which he agreed. Owing to the physical condition of the interpreters, it was necessary to reorganize the party as follows:-

'A' Party – Maritsa	'B' Party – Calatos
Capt. Allott	Lieut. Sutherland
Sgt. Moss	Sub.Lit. Calambokidis
Cpl. McKenzie	Mne. Duggan
Pte. Blake	Mne. Barrow
Kyrmichalis	Mne. Harris
	Savas

Lieutenant Calambokidis was kept by 'B' Party as he knew the area about Calatos, and as his knee would not stand the rough going to Maritsa. Captain Tsoucas was to remain in the area of the grotto and observe the result of the attack on Calatos, being picked up by myself on the night 13/14. Sergeant Moss was to proceed to Maritsa, as he alone could converse sufficiently with the guide in Italian. Before moving off, therefore, parties and equipment were organized and all surplus concealed.

Night 7/8.   Captain Allott's party moved off 2030 hours and I arranged that I would meet him at our first hideout on the night 16/17, all being well. Owing to the fact that I never saw Captain Allott or any of his party again, the rest of the report concerns the activities of 'B' party entirely.

The party moved off at 2100 and had considerable difficulty in finding water in the valley below, all apparent irrigation channels in the gardens being dry. The source was eventually found at about 0300. Crossing the road by the Malona bridge, the party proceeded to a lying-up position in the wooded hills to the west.

Night 8/9.   My plan was to move along the side of the hills nightly towards Calatos, observing the aerodrome defences from various angles on the route. This I could do slowly, moving short distances each night, as there was plenty of time in hand. After water had been collected from Malona village, the party moved on to the next hideout due west of the village of Massari, lying up that night and the following day in the dry bed of a torrent, sheltered from the north wind, which was especially cold at night. In the evening of the 9th I observed positions and movement in the valley between Massari, Castro Feraclo and Calatos.

Night 9/10.   Party moved down towards Massari, and waited for the guide and Marines Duggan and Harris to fetch water from Malona. As there was a civilian curfew at 2200 they had to enter the village shortly before this hour; on this and subsequent occasions none of the party were approached by the inhabitants. Party then proceeded towards Calatos at 2350 along the flat ground: a monastery was passed with a well on the north side. The position of this was noted for future reference. Ascending the hills again, the party lay up in another dry stream bed approximately 2 miles from the aerodrome with a good O.P. nearby, from which all persons observed the positions of dispersed aircraft and activity in the Calatos area throughout the following day. Great difficulty was experienced by all in sleeping at night due to the cold.

Night 10/11. As there was a very strong north wind, it was essential to find adequate shelter for sleeping that night. I observed a shepherd's cave about half a mile towards Calatos on the far side of the dry bed of the River Scatulari, which had a certain amount of straw visible through the entrance. I decided to get as much sleep as possible there, and then move on to a final OP before dawn. The water party moved off and joined us in the cave about midnight. In spite of the straw and shelter from the wind, it was still extremely cold and little sleep was obtained. Party moved off about 0500 and reached a final OP in the hills before dawn. This was a well-concealed place overlooking the aerodrome which was about 1 mile distant. I decided to observe all that day and make my plan the following evening.

Night 11/12. The water party left at dusk and returned about 2300, together with two shepherds who were friends of the guide. The latter had apparently made previous arrangements to meet them by the monastery. These men talked at length with Calambokidis and gave valuable information concerning the state of morale, etc, on the island, and pointed out various defences. They also brought fruit, cheese and bread, which was much appreciated. My plan was to attack the aerodrome in two parties and withdraw independently. The shepherds were sent off to search for a convenient hiding place near this RV, with instructions to meet both parties there and guide them into Mount Elias after the operation. They were also to supply us with fruit and water for the following day. The rest of the 12th was spent in observation with telescope and binoculars, until each member of the party knew the actual positions of the dispersed aircraft to be attacked and the nature of the defences to be overcome.

1. The author in 1941.

2. (Above left) "Douglas Pomford, a
   Golden Gloves champion" (p.37).

3. (Above) Mike Kealy: "great military
   authority behind his soft-spoken
   manner" (p.41).

4. (Left) "Kabrit Camp was full of
   interesting characters" (p.51).

5. "The 10-ton motor-boat *Porcupine*, commanded by John Campbell, one of the great SOE skippers of the war" (p.64).

6. HM Submarine *Traveller* (see p.71 *et seq*).

7. "One larger-than-life character in the SAS in those days was Paddy Mayne" (p.51).

8. David Stirling in pensive mood. He was "a long-range strategic thinker" (p.97).

9. The busts of Savas and Kyrmichalis (see p.93).

The aircraft were dispersed in such a way along the north-east side of the landing-ground as to afford an excellent target for a party of three men approaching across the dry bed of the River Gaddura and through the wire the other side. In this area there were three SM 84s, five Macci 202s and six CR 42s close together, and presumably guarded by only a few men, with more aircraft dispersed among the olive trees to the north-west. The rest of the SM 84s, some seventeen in number, were inside the aerodrome towards Calatos village, more widely dispersed but better guarded.

My plan was therefore as follows:- two parties would enter the aerodrome and attack simultaneously. 'A' party on the left, Lieutenant Calambokidis, Marines Barrow and Harris, would cross the River Gaddura, pass through the wire and attack all planes on the north-east side of the aerodrome working up towards the north-west.

'B' party, Marine Duggan and myself, would also enter the aerodrome from the same side, but further to the north-west, and continue towards Calatos attacking planes in the shelters and on the landing ground itself. I considered this plan to be as foolproof as possible since:-

(a) All five could not enter at one point.
(b) With two parties there was a double chance of success.
(c) 'A' party had a small area and many targets, which indicated the use of three men. Also, there was a better chance of escape in the direction from which they entered.
(d) 'B' party's targets were widely dispersed in the centre of the aerodrome. Two men could move more quickly here, with less chance of being detected. In case of the alarm being given, two men had a better chance than three of slipping through the defences.

Bombs were made ready and distributed, twenty-two to 'A' party and fifteen to 'B' party, the Bergens were dumped and spare water-bottles and kit sent back to the RV with the guide. Zero hour for placing the first bomb was to be 2359 hours. After the operation, parties were to withdraw separately to the RV. Whoever arrived there first was to wait for the other party till 0400 when they were to start for the hills to lie up the next day.

Calambokidis and myself gave much thought to all eventualities which might occur during the attack, and all three Marines clearly understood the timings and routes both in and out.

Night 12/13. Party moved off at 2015, reached a point about 300 yards from the main road and halted till 2245. The night was very dark with heavy rain. The road was crossed at 2255 and the parties separated in the dry bed of the River Gaddura at 2315. 'B' party heading south-east. From that moment onwards I never saw any of 'B' party again.

Marine Duggan and myself approached the north-west corner of the aerodrome and arrived within 100 yards of our first target at 2345. The plane was guarded, but the sentry moved off just before midnight. We moved in and placed bombs on this and two other SM 84s nearby. We crossed the wire and A/T ditch at approximately 0020 and walked down a path between buildings towards the landing ground. This was our only way into the aerodrome and the most direct route for the next attack. I identified our target and made towards it; we were, however, challenged by a sentry directly ahead who came towards us. We withdrew the way we had come, but he ran after us and shouted towards a lighted building on our right. I had no wish for the alarm to be given at this early stage, which would compromise 'A' party, and so recrossed the A/T ditch and wire. Various persons were heard moving about the aerodrome side of the ditch and seemed to remain patrolling the area. Since there was a curfew for all people except guards moving about the aerodrome, this entrance would be watched. I therefore decided to search for targets on our side of the ditch. A dump of petrol was found and bombs placed, but apart from that no other targets were apparent. I therefore placed the remainder of the bombs on the three SM 84s previously attacked, so as to leave no doubt as to their destruction.

As it was now well after 01.20 we withdrew slightly, hoping to contact 'A' party on their withdrawal. There being no sign, we moved off towards the RV just before 0200. At approximately 0210 our first bomb went up, followed shortly by the other two, and 15 minutes later the first of 'A' party's bombs exploded. This was followed by frequent explosions and a red glow spread over the sky above the 'drome. Owing to the fact that we were in a hollow the actual fires were not visible, but on reaching the RV at 0330 some twelve to fifteen fires were seen burning fiercely, and the explosions of the bombs and burning ammunition, and of material in the vicinity of the planes, were continuous. The targets were so close together that it was likely that they set each other ablaze.

The enemy unfortunately seemed to understand it to have been a ground attack, as searchlights swept the beach of Malona Bay and the low ground over the route of our withdrawal. At approximately 0350 two short bursts of machine-gun fire were heard, followed by what I thought was a short burst from a TSMG, coming from the foothills north-west of the aerodrome. These were accompanied by flashing of lights. I waited for 'A' party till 0430 and then decided to climb into the hills to lie up next day. The shepherds having already left, Marine Duggan, Savas and myself set off. We had left little time in which to be concealed before dawn and were hampered by the attentions of a searchlight flashing on us from the beach east of the aerodrome. The guide refused to go on whilst in the vicinity of the beam and stopped so frequently that he eventually had to be left behind, Marine Duggan and I proceeding alone into some rough ground. The guide being quite capable of hiding himself, I was not anxious as regards his safety.

Duggan and I lay up on the 13th and observed the result of the damage on the aerodrome. The remains of burnt-out planes were plainly visible, but difficult to count, being near to the ground and close together. There was much activity among the ground staff clearing up wreckage in the area. No enemy troop movements were visible in our vicinity. My intention now was to contact Captain Tsoucas and remain two days in the grotto, thence proceeding to the beach. As we had no food between us, having left the surplus with the guide, I did not, however, wish to be forced to go there before the night of 15/16.

Night 13/14, Duggan and I moved up the mountain to try and contact Captain Tsoucas, whom we fortunately located in an OP directly above where we had been lying up. He said that he had enough food and water to last us one day in his hideout near the cave where we spent the first night ashore. We accordingly proceeded there to lie up the next day. His observation report on the attack confirmed my own, but visibility was bad due to low cloud and rain. I therefore concluded that some thirteen to fifteen planes had been destroyed. He also reported hearing two explosions on the morning of the 13th. About 0930 the same morning a large aeroplane landed, remaining surrounded by people who came towards it from all sides of the 'drome before taking off about forty-five minutes later. This might have been used to carry away prisoners, had any of 'A' party been captured. A shepherd who brought water daily to Captain Tsoucas reported having found a haversack containing five water-bottles in the hideout where the Maritsa and Calatos parties separated. As Captain Allott took all available bottles this remains a mystery, but might indicate that Kyrmichalis, who was responsible for obtaining water, had been captured in this area.

Captain Tsoucas' hideout was badly situated as it was on a low hill facing the chapel of St Giorgio Lacomata, but, since there were no troop movements in the valley that day, I decided to remain there and proceed to the beach on the night of 15/16.

Night 14/15. Duggan and I tried to get through the wired-off portion of the beach north of Castro Feraclo and get water from the well behind the village of Caraci. The posts supporting the wire were painted white and, though I had seen no movement within this area, I did not believe it to be mined. Shortly after getting through the outside fence, I felt with my leg a thin wire stretched across the path; on examination I found this led to a metal canister standing about 8 to 10 inches high, which appeared recently laid and of a type similar to those used by the Italians in the Western Desert. It could therefore be concluded that all beaches suitable for landing were heavily mined. It was out of the question to go further, so I proceeded towards Malona and filled up with water in the gardens near the main road, the state of Duggan's boots not permitting the journey.

At approximately 1500 the next day a body of some thirty people were seen advancing in file towards us across the valley from the direction of Massari. These were identified as about twenty-four soldiers and six civilians. About 1,000 yards from our position they split in two, one party going to the left towards our beach and the other heading straight for us. We therefore quickly gathered what kit we had ready and ran over the crest on to the flat ground above the cliffs, keeping as close as possible to the foot of Mount Elias. We had a fair start and so rested in a small cove near the foot of the mountain. Captain Tsoucas protested that he could not go further owing to his physical condition, but I urged him to climb a steep slope to get higher, as this cave was too obvious a hiding place. We eventually arrived on a small sloping ledge fairly high up the mountain with a wall behind, overlooking a shepherd's hut, but did not have time to conceal ourselves before a number of small parties came round the foot of the mountain from the direction of Arcangelo. Thus only by a few minutes had we avoided the second arm of the pincer. Our only chance was to lie flat on this slope and hope that they would not search as high up as we were. The parties spread out and combed the low ground in front of us, each party having a civilian to act, presumably, as guide. Fortunately we were in the shade and not too conspicuous, nevertheless in the open. Parties then started coming up the mountain accompanied by much talking and shouting. The topmost one passed, fortunately, about 10 to 15 yards below us, and then moved down towards the flat ground above the cliffs. They apparently thought that we would not have time to climb any distance up the mountain and resumed their patrolling of the ground below.

At approximately 1730 a small motor-boat was observed approaching from the direction of Lindos; this patrolled close inshore towards Cap Arcangelo, where she hove to for some minutes and was identified as an MTB probably of the Baglietto type. Proceeding slowly back towards Lindos following the coastline, she eventually disappeared beneath the cliff somewhere in the neighbourhood of our beach and shut off her engines. As she approached, a small body of troops was observed on the fo'c'sle, presumably a small landing party. Some twenty minutes later, at about 1815, she started up and made off towards Lindos towing three black objects astern, which were easily identified as our rubber floats. The search parties continued to move about until dusk, when they dispersed, some towards Calatos and the rest towards Arcangelo.

It seemed therefore that someone of the party had been captured, probably one of the guides who was forced into giving away the place of landing, or that some shepherd had seen us and then spoken, hoping for a reward, though this is unlikely, owing to the universal hatred of the Italians. The outlook was therefore completely changed; we were without food and without means of re-embarkation. Moreover, I and the two with me might well be the only members of the expedition who knew the beach was guarded, and above all it might be too dangerous for the submarine to approach on the night of 17/18. I therefore decided to remain where we were and observe activity the following day.

Night 15/16. No activity that night or the following day, except occasional patrolling A/C. A very uncomfortable day was spent due to no food and being in the sun for ten hours without water. My intention for the following night was firstly to prevent any party from proceeding to the beach, and secondly to obtain from the cave a signalling torch and Mae Wests for our swim to the submarine.

Night 16/17. All being quiet, at 2000 our party moved down the mountain to a water trough near the shepherd's hut and filled up water-bottles. On re-ascending to the flat ground, Captain Tsoucas was left with our haversacks whilst Marine Duggan and I went to the cave. The following message was left tied to a signalling torch: 'Boats captured, signalling and swimming from intended landing place.' We waited there till 2330 and then started to move back, carrying one signalling torch and three Mae Wests. At this moment shouting in Italian was heard and flashing of torches observed in the area where we had left Captain Tsoucas. We advanced in that direction and got as close as possible to observe and listen. It was clearly apparent that a strong enemy force was in position covering the ground between the mountain and the cliff, between us and Captain Tsoucas, their intention being to waylay Captain Allott's party should they come down to the beach from the Arcangelo direction. To get round or through this patrol was out of the question due to visibility and the noisy nature of the going.

I, however, found a space under a large rock capable of accommodating two people and fairly well concealed; beside this we sat and observed till dawn. At first light I could clearly see about thirty to forty men collecting about 400 yards away, talking and shaking out their greatcoats prior to moving off. At dawn they split, one body moving off towards Cap Arcangelo and the other heading straight towards us. We therefore crept under the rock and prepared to lie up for the day. Another party came up from the Calatos direction and the whole area was thoroughly searched throughout the morning. Fortunately they did not find us, even though one man sat for five minutes on the rock a few feet above our heads. Great discomfort was experienced throughout the day, again without food and water and lying in an extremely cramped position. A portion of the ground above the cliff was in view to us and across this soldiers in various groups passed in both directions throughout the morning. At about 1330 a large body moved towards Calatos, headed by two officers, and carrying full equipment and MGs.

At 1405 four rifle shots were heard in the neighbourhood of the cave where we had left the message, followed shortly after by a revolver or Biretta shot, and accompanied by much shouting. All the troops in the area seemed to move in that direction and disappeared out of sight. Apart from a few voices near us in the afternoon, the rest of the day was quiet. My intention for the following night was to get to our beach before the night patrol was in position, there pick up Captain Tsoucas as previously arranged and carry on to the south-west.

Night 17/18. Moved off at 2000, rested and watered at the trough, arrived at beach where we had originally proposed to land at 2040. No sign of enemy patrols; Captain Tsoucas did not appear, so I sent Duggan to search towards Cap Arcangelo in case he had missed the position. He returned at 2115 having seen no one. I therefore thought that he would see our signals and join up later. First three groups of the letter K sent out at 2130. Duggan thought he saw recognition directly seawards, but could not be certain (it was in fact flashed through the periscope as submarine was still submerged). I waited till 2200 and received the recognition from submarine, replied, 'Y' and followed with the words, 'Swimming; come in'. The submarine was not visible through the binoculars when we entered the water directly afterwards. We swam for about an hour in the direction of the recognition signal until we heard the sound of engines; this I believed to be the submarine as I had previously been informed by Captain Allott that the ship's engines would be running to enable the party to locate her more easily. Duggan gave occasional flashes with the torch, but the sound grew fainter and eventually disappeared. I later found out from the Captain of HMSub. *Traveller* that these were the engines of the Italian MTB which attacked us just after we got on board. We were rather despondent at hearing what we thought was the submarine apparently going away, but encouraged each other to continue. In spite of the calm sea, our physical condition for such a swim was hardly adequate, owing to the recent strain, added to the fact that we had only had one tin of sardines each during five days, and little water. We were, however, determined to reach the submarine in spite of the growing cold, and much to our relief sighted her slightly to our right at about 2320. We were helped onto the fore planes and were inboard by 2330.

I explained to the Captain the situation ashore and the unlikelihood of any others being re-embarked. Since he had no further signals, and in view of the fact that we were in dangerous waters, the sub crash-dived to avoid two depth-charge attacks from the Italian MTB waiting for us. He forthwith set a course for Beirut.

I was exhausted and slept during most of our passage to

Beirut in a comfortable bunk. For no apparent reason my temperature began to fluctuate. The Medical Officer said, 'I think you should go to hospital in Beirut. I will arrange that for you.' There was a car waiting at the submarine base. Before leaving *Traveller* it was exciting and reassuring to see the submarine's 'Jolly Roger' flying at the masthead in a stiff breeze with the symbol for a successful Special Forces 'pick up' – a white dagger – proudly sewn on.

In hospital I noticed I had lost 15 lbs. Doctors were a bit baffled by my change in temperature, but soon pinned it down correctly to malaria, for which they had all the right drugs.

★   ★   ★

Recently Commander Michael St John, who had joined the Submarine Service direct from Dartmouth, told me he had detailed written instructions for the pick-up on 17 September. This involved the difficult manoeuvre of turning the submerged *Traveller*, with a crew of seventy, round with her stern towards the shore. This took a long time, but was vital to ensure a quick getaway. Looking through the periscope during the day, he saw no enemy activity on Rhodes. At 2130 exactly he saw through the periscope a signal from the beach which he acknowledged, also through the periscope. He did not know how many of the raiding group of twelve were being re-embarked. After about an hour two swimmers were spotted, hauled quickly on board and taken below. Half-naked and dripping wet, Marine Duggan and I were handed the largest and most welcome mugs of Naval Rum we had ever had. I began to tell the unflappable Michael St John the sad story of what had happened on shore. At that point *Traveller* crash-dived to avoid two depth-charge attacks. It is just as well that Duggan and I were safely on board, otherwise we would have been split open by the force of the depth-charges and our mangled bodies found floating in the sea next morning by the triumphant Italians. We avoided this ugly fate by a hair's breadth: I believe there were powerful hidden counter-forces, including *le bon Dieu*, at work to preserve our safety.

★   ★   ★

After the attack Governor-General Admiral Campioni wrote to Rome, saying:

> 'The first alarm, it appears at the moment, was given by a sentry at the Gaddura base, who reports the following: "I had the feeling that there was someone around the plane. I approached and saw a white dog come out from under a plane. I returned my rifle to the rest position, when suddenly I saw two men with a pistol aimed at me, who said in perfect Italian, 'Quiet, or we'll kill you.'"
>
> 'The soldier reports that he fainted [!] from the sudden emotion. When he came to, not much later, he says that he ran to the officer who commanded the platoon, whose tent was about 150 metres away, and reported what had happened. Almost immediately the explosions began on the field.
>
> 'So that, even though the night was dark and rainy, and the zone to be guarded was large, if the sentries had been doing their duty properly, I believe, they should have heard or seen something.
>
> 'Given that the regiment had charge of virtually all security services, and bearing in mind the importance of the objectives to be guarded, there ought to have been precise written instructions on the manner of executing the service, which did not exist.
>
> 'The Aegean national who was with them, (conductor on the bus service on the island of Rhodes, having been expatriated in November), may have been a good guide, but was certainly not in possession of the data gathered on the camp which made it possible to choose the easiest and most productive sector to operate. The possibility of someone operating from the inside cannot therefore be completely

dismissed. The investigations completed to date have given no confirmation of the above possibility.

'It seems from a receipt found on the Aegean that their provenance was Beirut, not Alexandria.

'Day and night patrols continue searching the island for the patrol which operated at Maritsa. Sufficient measures have been taken at sea to attack the submarines that come to take off the patrols. The arrested declare that they do not form part of the organization of the "Commandos". Ten "commandos", of which some "marines", left Beirut the 31st of August on the Greek submarine *Papanikolis*.

'According to General von Veldar, the same explosives were used for the two sabotage operations on airfields in Crete, June, 1942.

'The regulations that governed, both in general and particular, the organization of security of the airport, and fixed the precise mode of their execution, were found defective by the Officer in charge of the investigation. However, daily verbal agreements were made by the Commander of the camp and the command of the infantry regiment relating to the variable disposition of the aircraft on the field.

'The night of the 18th an enemy submarine was seen and attacked without success by one of our Mas, in the proximity of the bay of Arcangelo.

'From the declarations of the Aegean citizens, who took part in the expedition, they were to re-embark on an English submarine of the most recent type, from the night of the 17th to the night of the 19th (the Italian says the nights *to* the 18th and *to* the 20th) of September. The morse signals agreed were:

from land: dash dot dash
from sea: series of dots

'Of the two enemy patrols operating on Maritsa and Gaddura, the following have been captured to date:

90

2 English Captains, of which one of Greek origin;

1 Sublieutenant from the Greek marine;

1 English Sergeant;

1 Corporal and three soldiers, English;

The two Aegean nationals clandestinely expatriated from Rhodes in November, 1941, and enrolled in the Greek formations of the Near East.

'One Lieutenant and one soldier are still missing. Search parties are still trying to capture them.'

I needed time, comfort and space in order to write my report on Operation ANGLO. I took a double room on the top floor of Shepheard's Hotel, Cairo, so I could spread out papers and maps quietly, with restaurant and bar *sur place*. To my surprise I ran into Bernard Fergusson in the foyer looking for a room. He was in Cairo searching for volunteers for the next Wingate expedition. I offered him the spare bed in my room which he accepted. He looked thin. We dined and discussed the trials and tribulations of operating behind enemy lines.

For me, Operation ANGLO was one of the most hair-raising experiences imaginable. It was also a voyage of self-discovery. I learned that if one keeps one's head and nerve and uses the ground properly it was possible to survive in an enemy-infested area. Also, to take on such a difficult task in rugged country one must be better prepared and trained in heavy load-carrying, which I was not.

★   ★   ★

After the war I was a student at the Staff College, Camberley, in 1949. In April I received a letter from Aubrey Baring of the banking family and head of the Mayflower Film Production Company. He said he had heard about my long swim from Rhodes from his brother Evelyn, who had been on the

SAS operational planning staff during the war. He wondered if I would be interested in having a film made of the Rhodes raid. I was intrigued by his novel idea, coming, as it did, out of the blue. I soon found myself lunching with Aubrey Baring and his partner Maxwell Setton at the company office in Wardour Street. From the start it was clear that Aubrey Baring was keen to make the film and had made some preliminary arrangements. He had lined up the American Director Lewis Milestone, who knew how to make war films. Maxwell Setton asked where I thought the film should be made. I replied, 'Cyprus, where the land is similar, with a large garrison without much to do, ready and happy to be employed as extras.' I sent a copy of my operational report for them to give to the script-writer, Robert Westerby. The film was made in Cyprus. To ensure there were no 'military mistakes', I asked Walter Milner Barry, who had been in SBS during the war, to go to Cyprus and be technical adviser, which he was pleased to do. The film emerged in 1953 as *They Who Dare*, with a high-powered cast of actors. Dirk Bogarde took my part, Denholm Elliot was marine Duggan, and Akim Tamiroff played George Tsoucas. There was an interesting mistake. It is dangerous to crunch the end of a time delay with one's teeth to activate it. If Dirk Bogarde had done this for real, his distinguished career would have abruptly ended years ago when bursts of the sulphuric acid thus released hit his tummy. The film had mixed reviews. Over the years, however, it has done quite well, particularly in Japan where the men must like the look of the comely nightclub singer in the opening scene!

★   ★   ★

For some time the civic, religious and military authorities in Rhodes have been toying with the idea of placing at a prominent spot in the Old City statues of Nicolas Savas and George Kyrmichalis, local Operation ANGLO heroes. They were young – twenty-four and nineteen – ticket collectors on the Italian bus service on the island before and during the last war. They were fed up with the irksome life under the large Italian garrison and decided to do their bit for Greece and the Allied cause by joining the Greek army, at a moment in the war when things were going badly for the Allies. It meant getting from Rhodes to Egypt.

On the night of 13 November, 1941, Savas, Kyrmichalis and a friend, Tsapatsis, left Rhodes for Turkey. They rowed a stolen fishing boat. The Turks were pleased to see them but did not allow them to land. They went on rowing south past Castelrosso, Savas's home island. Villagers gave them food and water. After some days' rowing they decided to sink the boat, swim ashore and appear on land as shipwreck survivors. This they did and began walking towards the Turkish/Syrian border, picking up food as they went along. After walking roughly 400 kilometres they reached Selefkia. From there they went by bus and train, escorted by Turkish police, to the Syrian border. There they were met by the British, who sent them to Haifa. There on 14 February, 1942, they presented themselves to the Greek garrison, three months after leaving Rhodes. They were enlisted as private soldiers and given some weapon training.

In July, 1942, they volunteered to take part in Operation ANGLO as guides. Both were captured by the Italians, charged with treason and found guilty. Savas was executed on 7 October, 1942. Because of his youth, Kyrmichalis was spared but sentenced to life imprisonment, sent to a prison in Italy near Siena, and placed in solitary confinement. In 1944, after the Italian surrender, he was sent to Cairo. There he was diagnosed sick with tuberculosis and returned to his village, Soroni, where he died on 15 August, 1949.

On 1 September, 1996, I received a letter from Mr Emmanuel Papaioannou, Chairman of the Association of Rhodian Studies. He said the statues of Savas and Kyrmichalis would be unveiled on 6 October, 1996, and kindly invited me to attend, which I did. There is a lot of interest in Rhodes about

Operation ANGLO from local historians and the public. The raid was the only one of its kind in the Dodecanese at that black moment in the war for us. Burning planes lit up the night sky and were visible for miles. It cheered people up. They felt that, at last, the flame of resistance had been lit. Since 1985 I have been in touch with George Vroohos, lawyer and historian in Rhodes, who is the local expert on Operation ANGLO. At his invitation I visited Rhodes in November, 1986. I looked over the deadly open ground near Mount Elias, thanked Mr M. Papageorgiou of Malona for keeping the knowledge that we were on the island away from the Italians, put flowers on George Kyrmichalis' grave and had a memorable fish lunch with the Kyrmichalis family at a restaurant nearby.

Since then George Vroohos has written a book about Operation ANGLO, published by the Municipality of Rhodes in 1988. I have had this translated into English by two kind Greek ladies. It is an interesting read.

This programme for Sunday, 6 October was well organized by Mr Papaioannou, with a full sung mass at Rhodes Cathedral, the Bishop presiding. I noticed many immaculately turned-out Scouts and Guides near the altar rails and a full military guard of honour in place. We walked to where the statues were placed under an ancient tree, with traditional pebble-work underfoot. The Major-General Commanding Rhodes removed the statue covers and I gave an address, which was translated by Tassos Anthonlias, in which I gave an outline of the raid and the part played in it by Savas and Kyrmichalis.

★　　★　　★

There are four SAS super-heroes remembered with statues: Nicolas Savas and George Kyrmichalis, Greek Army Privates in Rhodes, for their part in Operation ANGLO, September, 1942; also in Rhodes, Stefan Casulli, Greek Army Lieutenant killed on the highly successful raid on the Island of Santorin

94

in April, 1943, and Anders Lassen, though Danish a Major in the British Army and the only SAS VC of the last war. He died in April, 1945, in circumstances of unbelievable gallantry, leading a major diversionary attack at Lake Comacchio on the east coast of Italy. His statue is outside the Resistance Museum, Copenhagen. There is a copy in one of the SAS Reserve Army Drill Halls in Scotland, near where he received Commando training as a young man.

The motivation of all these exceptional men was 'Patriotism'.

10

SBS Reorganization and Operation Albumen

June, 1943

In retrospect it is clear that there were four interrelated events which caused SBS reorganization: casualties, the Battle of Alamein, David Stirling's capture and the need for a role change. In 1942 we had unexpectedly heavy losses. Captain Grant Watson was drowned in March trying to reach a German plane that had crashed on an island near Gazala Point. On 11 August George Duncan, Desmond Buchanan, Eric Newby, Sergeant Dunbar, Corporals Booth, Butler and Duffy were landed in Sicily from HM submarine *Una* to attack a German bomber base threatening an important convoy. An account of this raid is in Eric Newby's book *Love and War in the Apennines*. They ran into an alert enemy and were all captured. Later in August another SBS group were briefed to land at Daba, quite close behind the German defences opposite Alamein, to attack the landing strip there. There was a fierce fight and Corporal Gurney was wounded so badly that he could not move, and Michael Alexander remained with him, both men being taken prisoner.

Then in September there was Operation ANGLO, successful but expensive. Of the twelve who landed only two returned. Also, sadly, Major Tom Montgomery was killed in a jeep crash on his way to give us the latest intelligence on Rhodes before we left on ANGLO.

In the spring of 1942 the Unit War Establishment of SBS

was thirty-five officers, non-commissioned officers and men. In December, 1942, there were only two SBS officers still in action, Tom Langton and myself, plus a dozen of the irrepressible 'original' NCOs and men. The second half of 1942 saw a tussle for control of the SBS between Michael Kealey and David Stirling. Michael was a traditional operator in the Roger Courtney mould, while David wanted to absorb the SBS into his expanding SAS. As SBS casualties rose, so the pressure increased for an SAS take-over. This development suited me because I felt the original SBS role of beach reconnaissance and short-side sabotage had been overtaken by strategic events in the Mediterranean. In November, 1942, Michael left for England where he had a distinguished career in the SBS there and in the Far East.

In his book *The Special Air Service* Philip Warner says, 'The SBS was too hazardous a service to remain intact for long'. This is correct. Looking back, 1942 was a year of continual crisis for us as the war was going inexorably the Germans' way. For this reason, SBS operations were planned in a hurry with little preparation, thought or training.

The strategic situation changed dramatically in our favour following General Montgomery's victory at the Battle of Alamein, which began on 23 October, 1942. Within a month Rommel's Army had been pushed back to El Agheila. David Stirling was a long-range strategic thinker. Around mid-December I heard that a large-scale SAS operation was planned in the Tunisian frontier area involving David himself. Having nothing much to do, I bearded him in his Kabrit office, angry at being left out. He turned on me, eyes flashing. 'You are not going and I'll tell you why. You, George Jellicoe and Tom Langton have unique small boat operational experience. You will be needed soon to carry out raids on the soft underbelly of Europe. You are much too valuable to be wasted elsewhere.' And with that ringing in my ears I saluted and left.

Little did any of us realize that it would be the end of the war in Europe, two and a half years away, before we saw David Stirling again. General Rommel cleverly set up a special unit with the specific task of tracking down and dealing with the SAS, for which he provided unlimited finance. It worked. On 24 January, 1943, Stirling and a group of SAS were surrounded near the Gabes Gap in Tunisia and forced to surrender. In due course he was sent to Colditz where he met Commandant Bergé, leader of the French SAS raid on Heraklion airfield, and Michael Alexander. The latter, as we have seen, was captured on the Daba raid in August, 1942. He was given a rough time by the German interrogators who said they might execute him under the terms of Hitler's Commando Order. Being a quick-thinking man, Michael said, 'My uncle, General Alexander, is the commander-in-Chief and it would be most unwise of you to execute me.' The Germans deferred and sent him to Colditz. Never in the history of name-dropping has there been such a rich reward!

There was some confusion at Kabrit when the news of Stirling's capture broke because he carried many of the future plans in his head. I remember the Adjutant, Captain Blyth, sitting glumly at his desk piled high with files. It was obvious to us all that Stirling should be succeeded by the redoubtable Paddy Mayne, which is what happened. 2 SAS, commanded by David Stirling's brother William, was already operating successfully in Tunisia and planning operations in Sicily and Italy. In a reorganization which took place at that time, Mayne's SAS became known as the Special Raiding Squadron (SRS). The SRS was used successfully in the invasion of Sicily and Italy in July and September, 1943. The SBS was also enlarged and reorganized to undertake raids into the Aegean from a base in Palestine.

The SRS was given a war establishment of 230 officers, non-commissioned officers and men, to include full operational planning, training and administrative back-up. The core of the unit were three Operational Detachments of sixty men, based on five patrols, ten strong, with a Headquarters and signal element. The unit was formed on 1 April, All Fool's Day, 1943. 'As good a day as any,' I recall George Jellicoe remarking when he took command. The three Detachments were named after their founders – 'L' Langton, 'M' Maclean and 'S' Sutherland. Towards the end of 1942 Fitzroy Maclean was sent to Persia to kidnap the pro-Axis Persian General Zahedi. This he did with typical panache. The soldiers he used for this amusing and important task, many of them Highlanders, were, in his view, just the right men for the SBS. They became the vigorous, incisive 'M' Detachment.

George Jellicoe made an imaginative choice in picking Athlit Bay as the SBS base in Palestine. Picture a crescent-shaped beach about a mile across with a ruined Crusader castle at one end, the sea turning azure in the changing sunlight and the steep Carmel Hills behind. It was an ideal base and training area for the kind of operations we expected to carry out. Tom Langton formed 'L' Detachment from officers and men at Kabrit who did not want to join Mayne and SRS. I did the same, but arranged to get the people I wanted to Beirut for a month's sea training and walking in the Lebanon mountains. Each man could handle a 10-ton sailing caique in moderate weather, move over, and conceal himself in, rough ground carrying a 40 lb load. I passed on my operation experience from Crete and Rhodes.

It was at that time that Kenneth Lamonby joined us. A young lieutenant from the Suffolk Regiment, whose parents lived near Ipswich, he knew all the East Anglian tidal rivers and was a dinghy expert. I put him in charge of sea training. At Athlit all the tents and camp stores were dumped in an enormous heap. We erected the tents carefully. Athlit, as a new camp, had a calm, purposeful feel about it, in direct contrast to Kabrit, which struck me as noisy, brash and slightly out of control. At Kabrit, because SBS was small and with a different role, we were sidelined a bit. At Athlit all this changed and at last, after two years in the SBS, I had time to think, plan teams and train for the operations ahead. I pinched a tent with a stunning westerly view of the sea for 'S' Detachment office. My memories of Athlit are full of the characters I met there, the rigorous training routine laid down by George Jellicoe, the incomparable Mediterranean climate and the strong sense of comradeship that developed within the unit.

The day began at 6.30 with a cup of tea; by this time the sun was well up, and 30 minutes fierce PT and swimming from the tireless instructor, 'Brown Body' Henderson, who came from Perth. The punishment was extra press-ups. Knowing I was in the Black Watch, he would stand over me and say, 'Now sir, five for the North Inch and five for the South Inch'. I fittened rapidly. Walter Milner Barry joined us from the Transjordan Frontier Force. He was older than we were, with a Shell Oil background in the Middle East, spoke Arabic and knew the importance of the diplomatic approach. Among his grey hairs there was much wisdom about the strategic and political aspects of SBS operations. He was an important foil to our simpler, even naive, impatience. At Athlit in the early days, among many valuable men, Jack Nicholson, who worked in the Peebles tweed mills, Douglas Pomford, John Laverick and Cree, Jenkins and Marshall of the Irish Patrol stood out.

Presiding over our widespread activities like a classical orchestral conductor was George Jellicoe. With patience, firmness and humour he managed to get the best out of us. The exercises he set us were monumentally difficult and testing. It was at this point that two high-grade Commando officers joined SBS from England, Philip Pinkney and Anders Lassen.

George Jellicoe told me that he had met Lassen shooting geese with William Stirling at Keir, liked him and asked General Laycock, Chief of Combined Operations, to have him sent to the SBS. He joined my Detachment as we were gearing up for a major five-day exercise involving marching from Athlit to Lake Tiberias and back, a distance of 100 miles under load at night, attacking various simulated targets on the way. I was chatting in my office with Jack Nicholson about the exercise when a jeep drove up. Out stepped a six-foot, well-built man with fair hair and blue eyes. Speaking with a guttural accent, he said, 'I'm Anders Lassen. I have come from England to join you.' There was something compelling about his movements and presence. I remember saying to him, 'Welcome to the SBS. We are delighted you are with us.'

As Nicholson was standing around, I said to Anders, 'Here is your Patrol Sergeant. I know you will get along well.' They did. On the test exercise, when we used American K rations for the first time, Lassen did extremely well. He floated effortlessly over the ground carrying a 50 lb Bergen. He memorized the map and arrived at the RV early. He outshot us all on the range. On another exercise south of Beirut he was running late for an important RV. He stopped a French military truck, threw the Senegalese driver into a ditch, got his men aboard the truck and made the RV. It took all of George Jellicoe's charm and diplomacy to calm down the furious French military!

Lassen was very impressive. He had spent his childhood on a large estate in the Danish countryside. He was familiar with the 'great outdoors' and used a knife and bow and arrow to kill deer. He was a seaman in the merchant marine on an oil tanker when the war started. When he stepped ashore in Britain in 1940 he asked to join the British Army, which he did. After Commando training in Scotland he joined March-Phillips, Appleyard and others as crew members on *Maid of Honour*, a fishing smack, to liberate some important secrets impounded in the Central West African port of Fernando Po. For his seamanship, sound judgment and quick thinking Lassen was awared the Military Cross. He fought the war from a different standpoint to others in the SBS, with the exception of Kyrmichalis, Casulli and

Mavrikis. Denmark was occupied by the Germans. Britain was not and never would be. I have often wondered if this accounted for Lassen's ferocity towards the Germans. This and fluent German made him a truly formidable SBS operator.

Philip Pinkney, another interesting character, suggested that we should use wild plants, flowers and insects to augment our meagre operational diet. He had us out one misty morning looking for slugs which he devoured with gusto. 'Full of essential protein,' he would say. I thought otherwise! A hilarious account of all this is found in John Verney's witty account *A Diet of Herbs*. Later Pinkney left us and joined the SAS. In September, 1943, he parachuted into Italy to attack railways south of Bologna. The operation was successful, but he was captured and shot.

I had been promoted Captain with the formation of 'S' Detachment. I wrote to my father who was delighted. My feelings were a mixture of excitement for the operations ahead, gratitude and privilege for having such a special group of men to lead.

The Raiding Force Middle East structure was in place with HQ at Assib on the Palestine coast north of Haifa, reporting to GHQ Cairo, and under command:

> SBS, Greek Sacred Regiment
> Levant Schooner Flotilla
> Later during 1943-LRDG.
> We wore the SAS Regimental badge and wings.

In the middle of July Fitzroy Maclean left the SBS and returned to London to become the Prime Minister's Political and Military Representative in Yugoslavia. This is covered in his wartime classic *Eastern Approaches*. His place was taken by Ian Lapraik, a Cameron Highlander who had risen to prominence in Abyssinia with the Middle East Commando.

Langton's health had lately deteriorated to such an extent

that he was invalided home, so John Verney took over 'L' Detachment.

The first operation under Jellicoe's command was in Crete. The task was to destroy enemy aircraft on three Cretan airfields which could be used to attack shipping supporting the Allied invasion of Sicily. As I had been to Crete the year before and knew the island and its problems, Jellicoe asked 'S' Detachment to undertake the operation. In previous years, 1941 and 1942, SBS operations were carried out with no written orders or radio communications. Now we had both. This was a timely development. The Operation Order to me and the SBS was signed by General Scobie for C-in-C MEF, dated 12 June, 1943.

Since three airfields some distance apart were our targets, my plan was to direct an officer-led patrol to each target and control the operation from a concealed stores dump near the landing beach. Lieutenant Lamonby had Heraklion, Lassen Kastelli and Rowe Tymbaki. Each patrol included a signaller and radio set and battery, together weighing some 65 lbs, to be carried in addition to the weapons, food, explosives and miscellaneous equipment needed for the task. On the night of 23 June ML 361 landed three officers, fourteen men and two guides. Rowe's Patrol joined us four days later. All equipment not immediately needed was hidden among boulders to the rear of the beach. The whole group then moved out through a narrow and precipitous gorge that was the only exit. Owing to the weight each man was carrying (70–80 lbs) the appalling nature of the country we were covering and the uncertainty of the guides, we did not reach the lying-up area till after daybreak and so had to move with great care during the first day.

Small caves were found in the hillside, a lying-up point found 500 metres away and positions overlooking the approaches located. I had a talk with Lassen and Lamonby as we sat in the shade, looking down on the still blue sea below with a rasping noise from the ubiquitous cicadas hidden in the oleander bushes. They were relaxed and keen. I remember saying to them, 'It is now 1710. D-day is 4 July. As the going is atrocious and you both have a long way to go, I think you should leave in the late afternoon and take advantage of some daylight.' To this they agreed. To save them unnecessary toil I took a small party to the beach and got extra rations and two batteries for the radio sets for them. I saw the two parties out of the base area and on their way.

They remained together for the first five nights, making slow and arduous progress over rock-strewn hills and along narrow gullies, which strained their muscles and drained their strength. Their only consolation was the kindliness and co-operation of all the Cretans they met. They provided food and water and occasionally helped with the loads. They provided information on local conditions and the possibility of running into enemy troops. Without Cretan support the SBS would never have reached their targets or been able to attack them. On approaching Heraklion Lamonby was told that the airfield had declined in importance to the Germans over the last year. Having been run down, it seemed, as a result of the French SAS and Jellicoe's attack, very few aircraft used the place and never flew at night. In these changed circumstances Lamonby decided there was no point in moving closer to Heraklion. So he moved to the village of Reze, where, he had been told, there was a large petrol dump. He and Lance-Corporal Holmes put a number of Lewes bombs among the petrol trucks, which destroyed them and set the whole dump on fire. After making this spectacular blaze, which accounted for between 150 and 200 tons of aviation fuel, they withdrew the thirty miles to the beach.

Lassen's patrol experienced the kind of hair-raising adventure which was soon to be recognized as the price to be paid for accompanying him on this kind of operation. The patrol arrived at Kastelli airfield on time, having left the exhausted signallers behind. They spent a day observing and getting information from the ever-helpful Cretans. Their main targets were eight Stukas at the south-west corner of the airfield and five JU 88s, a few fighters and other planes disposed elsewhere. All the planes were guarded, particularly the Stukas. Instead of attacking with his patrol concentrated, Lassen decided to follow the example I set on Rhodes and split his force. Half would cause a spectacular and noisy diversion which would enable Sergeant Nicholson and Corporal Greaves to carry out the main purpose of the raid without too much interference, while Lassen and Gunner Jones caused mayhem elsewhere. The plan worked well. Five aircraft were destroyed and Lassen, bluffing his way in by pretending to be a German officer, shot four sentries. There was a furious German reaction and the patrol was chased into the hills. Instead of dropping into a coma of exhaustion, which his activities during the previous hours, indeed days, might have warranted, Lassen was wide awake when the Germans began to search the area where he and Gunner Jones were lying up. They were able to hide in a nearby cave, without moving or food for three days, till their pursuers concluded they had got away and abandoned the search. Because of this delay Lassen and his patrol arrived at the dump the day before embarkation. Meanwhile Rowe and his patrol had landed. They marched to Tymbaki, only to find no German aircraft there, and returned to the dump furious and deeply disappointed.

Though the dump party and I had been spared the physical exhaustion of the overland marches, there was plenty to do while we waited for the operation to develop. The operation, ALBUMEN, was planned to last twenty days. My main worry was that we would be rumbled by the Germans before then. Every item of personal equipment – food, bedding, ammunition, radio batteries, weapons – all had to be concealed so that they were invisible by day. In my experience the German search parties would move by day and dominate the ground, and not by night, which presented danger and uncertainty for them. I had to organize day-long watches over the approach routes. This was boring, hot and uncomfortable, but vital, work. Also I had to keep an eye on how the operation was going through the signals traffic. We were lucky in having an excellent signaller in the shape of Sergeant Beagley. This was the first operation SBS had its own signals back-up. The base was outside Cairo with powerful transmitters and sensitive receivers. We used the fixed schedule system and for security the one-time pad. The patrol set was the battery-driven A Mk 2. The set was light but each battery weighed 25 lbs. As our problem was battery life, at the dump we used a captured Italian army battery charger to top up the batteries. This was curiously designed like a deckchair with pedals and chair linked to a small electric generator, but it worked. I spent a lot of time pedalling away and talking to the unflappable Sergeant Beagley, who had volunteered to come with us and was our only link with the outside world. In the late afternoon of D + 10 a message came in reporting success at Kastelli and Heraklion. Then silence, until suddenly during the afternoon of D + 13 Lamonby warned of imminent enemy patrol activity in the coastal sector nearby.

At dawn on 10 July Sergeant Nicholson and Corporal Greaves arrived at the dump, having returned independently with the guide from Kastelli. They were in fine form and said that Lamonby and the rest of their patrols were lying up two hours away. Lieutenant Nicholas Souris, the MO4 agent, arrived at 8 am and said that there had been a number of reprisals and about twenty-five Cretans were with Lamonby's and Lassen's patrols. These brave men had acted as guides on the approach march to our targets and, having left their villages, were compromised and would have to be embarked with us. Having been in Crete on a similar operation the year before, I realized the danger of keeping together a group of between twenty-five and fifty worried men lying up in the mountains near the sea six days after a sabotage attack. I therefore decided to send an immediate signal requesting re-embarkation the following night – a day early. At 1000 hrs Sergeant Beagley started transmitting: halfway through the message the set stopped for lack of power. The only thing to do now was to get batteries from patrols away from the dump and hope that by linking them in series there would be enough power to send the rest of the message. This meant sending out four men in two directions in daylight to get the batteries. They returned about 1450. The message was successfully passed at 1500 and confirmed at 1900. Luckily the German four-man patrol nearby, and unknown to us, did not spot us moving around to get the batteries.

As this was our last night on Crete I sent a runner to Lassen and Lamonby at 2100 ordering them, their patrols and all the Cretans to come to the dump. They arrived around midnight and lay up in the wooded gorge below the dump. I was thankful when they arrived and before going to sleep spent an hour talking to Lassen and Lamonby about what they and their patrols had done at Heraklion and Kastelli. They were truly impressive and I have so often thought how fortunate we were to have excellent officers and men in the SBS. It was, after all, their first operation.

Just after first light the lookout reported that Lieutenant Rowe and his patrol were approaching. They found the remainder in the gorge. They reported that they had been forced to move because they saw three Greek policemen and a German soldier moving around. I had guards posted at the appropriate spots, but no enemy movement was seen during the day.

As it was our last day on the island I had a large meal of porridge, cheese and biscuits, and sweet milky tea, then finished my bag of dates. At 1500 a message was received confirming that the ML had sailed at 0500 and was due at our beach at midnight. I then began preparations for re-embarkation. July is the hottest month of the year in Crete and that day it was like an airless furnace. No water was obtainable during the day and I had to restrain the parched Cretans from visiting all the water points in the area. The only thing to do was to lie stretched out in the shade waiting patiently for sundown.

With nothing much to do at this point in the operation, I went to sleep. The next thing I remember was my arm being squeezed and a quiet voice in my ear, 'keep still'. At about 2000 hrs two German soldiers had been spotted approaching up the gully. Men from Rowe's and Lassen's patrols scattered and lay in the rocks. Lamonby's patrol prevented the Cretans moving. The enemy eventually worked their way into our position, were surrounded and captured without a shot being fired. While the German prisoners were being searched, some of the Cretans saw two more Germans – the other half of the patrol – at the bottom of the gully. Being for once in their lives on more or less equal terms, they began firing at them. The Germans quickly withdrew towards the sea, pursued by some fifteen armed Cretans completely out of control, whereupon a miniature battle took place, the Germans having taken up positions with their backs to the sea. This lasted for about 45 minutes, during which time a considerable number of rifle and sub-machine gun rounds were exchanged. The Germans, by skilful use of ground and cover, had the better of the Cretans, who had poor weapons. The wind had died down and the noise of this skirmish must have been audible for miles up and down the coast. It would have been dangerous for us if news of our presence had been spread by telephone.

Since it was then 2045 and a strong north wind had been blowing all day the ML might not arrive for another six hours. I therefore sent Lamonby and four men down the gully to stop the firing! This was done in the end, but it was getting dark and two Cretans were left to prevent the Germans moving towards our re-embarkation beach. Lamonby sent the men back, but failed to return himself and I concluded that, as it was dark, he would go straight to the beach. At 2120, after final arrangements, I led the group to the beach, prisoners under strong guard, Cretans in the rear. Everything was done to facilitate a quick embarkation. As there was no sign of Lamonby I sent Lassen and his patrol with instructions to search the gully where he was last seen, shouting his name at regular intervals. He returned at 2345 with no sign of him.

At midnight we began the pre-arranged recognition signal, 'D's repeated every five minutes. Ten minutes later we heard the ship's engines, and ten minutes after that we began re-embarking. By one in the morning the re-embarkation was complete. At my request the ML steamed slowly round Cap Holmoxos and lay off the mouth of the gully in which Lamonby was last seen. There being no sign of him, the Captain set course for Matruh. Having stirred up a lot of trouble for the Germans on Crete, we expected to be attacked from the air next day on our return passage to Egypt, but for some reason this did not happen.

I was particularly concerned about Lamonby. Sitting below in the cool wardroom with Lassen and Rowe, we talked about him. As Lassen and his patrol had searched in vain for him last night and had experience of three operations with Special Forces raised in England before he joined us, I asked him what he thought had happened. He said, 'The fact that he could not make the re-embarkation beach and we could not find his body is a bad sign. I think he has been wounded and taken away by the Germans for interrogation.' With that realistic assessment Rowe and I agreed, but with deep regret.

During the day at sea, as ordered, I prepared a brief account of the result of Operation ALBUMEN for GHQ Middle East. It was sent by naval cypher over the MLS radio. In an immediate reply GHQ said they would like to see the two prisoners as soon as possible at CSDIC. The Combined Services Detention and Interrogation Centre, at Maadi near Cairo, had a rather tough reputation! Operations of the

ALBUMEN type were all about surprise and the use of ground. The two Germans were unlucky to be captured. They had approached slowly uphill from the sea and we saw them coming. If all four in the patrol had been moving quietly in the hills above and had spotted us from there, the outcome would have been very different. Also, there was the dramatic culture change – one day sunning oneself contentedly in Crete, the next facing hostile interrogators in Cairo. A certain sympathy between captors and prisoners, now known as the Stockholm Syndrome, developed.

Since for me it had been a relatively inactive, indeed sometimes boring, nineteen days on Crete, I felt it would be fun for everyone in the group, particularly those who had faced all the danger, if we all went to Groppi's Restaurant in Cairo for a celebratory session of coffee/tea, cakes and large ice-cream sodas. This novel idea received massive support!

We reached Matruh safely at 1845 on 12 July and tied up in the harbour. For the last hour I chatted on the bridge with Lieutenant Young, the Commander of ML 361, and Lieutenant Ramseyer who was there for the ride. I pressed the point that we all owed much to the professionalism and skill of Young and his crew. Three passages into enemy waters were successfully made. If we had not been re-embarked the future for all of us would have been grim. For me it was a feeling of intense relief that the operation, my sixth with SBS, was completed successfully. But it had lasted too long.

Twenty-five Cretans came out with us and were met at Matruh by MO4 representatives from Cairo. They soon piled into trucks with their few belongings and disappeared. All I wanted to do was wash, shave and sleep. As it happened there was a tented camp near the harbour run by the Navy. We spent the whole of the next day resting and cleaning up. The following morning, after a massive breakfast, we left Matruh for Cairo, a five-hour jeep journey.

Groppi's Restaurant, that fabulous travellers' haven, is near the Midan Suleiman Pasha in the centre of Cairo. I shall

10. "George Jellicoe made an imaginative choice in picking Athlit Bay as the SBS base in Palestine" (p.99). Here tents are being put up at the camp in April, 1943.

11. "Kenneth Lamonby... a young lieutenant from the Suffolk Regiment... was a dinghy expert" (p.99).

12. "Jack Nicholson, who worked in the Peebles tweed mills" (p.100).

13. The author relaxes with a pipe during Operation *Albumen* (see p.105 *et seq*).

14. "Lassen was very impressive" (p.101). He won the MC three times and, posthumously, the VC.

15. One of the German prisoners the author took to Groppi's in Cairo for tea, an act of hospitality unappreciated in certain quarters (see p.111).

16. Colonel Tsigantes,
Commander of the Sacred
Squadron: "Dark and short,
with a deeply lined face hidden behind sun-glasses"
(p.131).

17. "The crescent-shaped Castelrosso waterfront" (p.116).

18. "The Turks marched us up to Bodrum Castle and locked us up there while they checked our credentials" (p.147).

19. The author and Lord Jellicoe in front of the Special Forces Memorial in Athens in 1991.

never forget the look of astonishment and admiration on the faces of countless pretty girls sitting around waiting for something to happen. Anders Lassen, with the Military Cross ribbon on his left breast, looked sensational. We split up, taking various tables. Soon the eager waiters were taking our substantial orders. The two German prisoners had looked soulful on the sea passage from Crete but cheered up a bit at Groppi's! They wore shorts, but removed their Afrika Korps képis. Otherwise they looked like 'one of us'. We ate large quantities of everything on offer: coffee, tea, cakes, fruit, ice-cream sodas. Around 6 pm I thought it was time to get rid of the prisoners and send them under guard to CSDIC, which I did. We then finished for the day. I went to Shepheard's Hotel for the night, taking Lassen and Rowe with me.

Next morning on the telephone was the furious Commander of CSDIC. 'Sutherland, what do you mean by taking two German prisoners to Groppi's? They might have escaped. Your conduct is against the rules and insufferable.' I replied, 'Brigadier, it is rare for the SBS to take prisoners on operations in enemy territory. In this case we were obliged to treat them as normal human beings since we did not know if we were going to be re-embarked safely with them or not. This is why they participated in the Groppi's celebratory event, where we could keep a close eye on them. Also we handed them over in a positive, co-operative frame of mind for your interrogators to work on. You must appreciate, sir, that we in the SBS, due to our role, have a different code of conduct in these matters.' He said, 'I think this is all highly irregular. I will complain to your Commanding Officer.' He never did! I heard later that the two Germans gave some valuable intelligence on Crete. More significant, the two semi-automatic rifles they carried were, I was told, technically ahead of anything we had ourselves at that time.

As soon as we returned to Athlit I arranged a post mortem on Operation ALBUMEN. We went through the whole sequence of events in detail. We felt that, by and large, things had gone well, though the signallers needed more training in cross-country load-carrying. Our main concern was the loss of Kenneth Lamonby. I said I would write to his parents and tell them what had happened to him. This I did with a heavy heart because he was all that one admires in a young man – intelligent, adaptable and brave, with an earthy Suffolk sense of humour. He was wounded, as we had feared, and died in Heraklion Hospital. He is buried in the most beautiful and peaceful military cemetery imaginable at Suda Bay. He was our first casualty and died aged 22. Flowers are always on his grave.

11

With the SBS in
the Aegean

1943–44

After the rigours of Operation ALBUMEN I took a week's leave and drove to Alexandria for a complete change of scene and pace, and the pleasure of the company of Thessy Whitfield, her family and friends. It was incredibly hot and we spent much time on Sidi Bishr beach and by the Sporting Club pool. Thessy was looking more relaxed now the war was, at last, going our way. The invasion of Sicily had begun on 10 July and was making good progress. We had a couple of sensational *diners à deux* at the Union Bar, which I remember to this day. As I told my jeep driver to head home to Athlit, leaving sophisticated Alexandria behind, I had the contented smile of a lucky man.

The success of the Sicilian invasion, followed by clear signs that the Allies were actively preparing to invade Italy itself, prompted the Italian Government, headed by Marshal Badoglio, which was not too keen on getting involved in the war in the first place, to begin negotiating for an armistice. These secret negotiations with the Allies excluded the considerable German military presence throughout Italy and the Balkans. A short armistice was signed near Syracuse on 3 September, 1943, under the terms of which all Italian ground and air forces would lay down their arms when approached by Allied soldiers. In return for this, the Allies would guarantee kindly and sympathetic treatment for Italian troops and civilians. Although the Allies promised not to announce the terms for nine days, it was in fact made public on the evening of 8 September.

At this point someone in the planning staff at GHQ Cairo felt that the Armistice with Italy might provide a chance of getting some British forces into Rhodes while the Italians were deliberating and before the Germans acted. The idea was to dispatch to Rhodes a mission to rally and encourage the Governor, Admiral Campioni, his staff and the troops under their command to contain the German forces on the island. This would allow the disembarkation of British troops sent to their assistance, the capture of Rhodes and the subsequent domination of the Aegean by RAF planes based on Rhodes. The garrison on the island was 35,000 Italians and 10,000 Germans and the task of leading this difficult and dangerous mission was given to George Jellicoe. He dropped on Rhodes by parachute on the night of 9 September with MO4 Interpreter Major Dolbey and wireless operator Kesterton. Uncertain how he would be received before landing, Jellicoe ate the written message from General Wilson to Admiral Campioni! When he went to negotiate with Campioni, the unfortunate Admiral had learned of the armistice only 32 hours before. The German military believed they had been double-crossed and were furious. The commander of Storm Division Rhodes, General Klemann, sent troops to try and take over the three airfields, Maritsa, Calatos, and Cuthavia in the south. These moves were thwarted around Maritsa by loyal Italian artillery.

The Admiral and his staff were cheered by the unexpected British visitors. It seemed to him that the British would hardly commit a real 'English milord' – Jellicoe had succeeded to the title on the death of his father in 1935 when he was only 17 – to a project they did not intend substantially to underwrite, and he became enthusiastic at the prospect of what they would achieve in co-operation with British forces deployed in strength. The immediate landing of a British armoured Division, plus extra artillery and perhaps preceded by a strong airborne force dropped on Maritsa airfield, would, the Admiral proclaimed, transform the situation. The Admiral's staff nodded in agreement. How much time did they have before the assaulting forces arrived? This of course was the crux of the matter, and Jellicoe had to reveal that for at least six days only a few small bodies of Special Service troops would be available. They all decided to 'sleep on it'.

The following day was spent in an atmosphere of equivocation: German staff officers arrived and departed and Jellicoe's attempts to find out exactly what was happening were foiled either by genuine ignorance on the part of Campioni's staff or deflected by his protestations of sincerity. In the evening the Admiral reported that the situation had deteriorated rapidly in the afternoon. The Germans were about to move in strength into Rhodes town itself. He urged Jellicoe and Kesterton to leave Rhodes for Castelrosso as soon as possible after dark with the Chief of Staff, and placed an Italian MTB at their disposal. Dolbey, whose leg was broken on this his first parachute jump, had already been smuggled to Cyprus in an Italian seaplane with an interim report from Jellicoe. Not wishing further to embarrass the Governor, Jellicoe and Kesterton took his advice and left Rhodes for Castelrosso with the Chief of Staff, Colonel Farnetza, in the MTB provided.

The first time I learned of the Italian armistice was at midday on 9 September. I had just started lunch in the Athlit officers' mess when I was called to the telephone. It was the Duty Officer at Raiding Force HQ, Azzib. In an excited voice he said, 'The Italians have surrendered. Grab as many of your men as you can. Get them, weapons and equipment on board an ML in Haifa harbour and occupy the island of Castelrosso as soon as possible.' I asked where George Jellicoe was. 'In Cairo being briefed.'

I managed to dig out Walter Milner Barry, a dozen of my men who were snoozing on their beds and ten men from 'M'

Detachment. There was no one else about. We piled every-thing we thought we would need, weapons, ammunition, cooking kit, blankets etc, onto two 3-ton trucks and headed for Haifa harbour 20 miles away. The ML was fuelled, armed and ready for sea. As soon as we had stowed ourselves and our equipment below, the Captain came over and said, 'I would like to leave now. We will be sailing into a northerly gale and must refuel in Cyprus. Let us discuss later how you want to land on Castelrosso.'

The next couple of days are best forgotten in the demoral-izing grip of acute sea-sickness. The island of Castelrosso is lozenge-shaped! It seemed to me the best way of occupying it was to land on the southern beach at night and move north and take the harbour unexpectedly from the south. Milner Barry was completely impervious to sea movement. During the night he stood over me saying, 'David, what do you want to do, land on the open beaches or sail into the protected harbour?' It is not difficult to deduce which my answer was!

I came on deck at midnight and a morse conversation in halting Italian was going on between the ML and the two Italian forts guarding the port entrance. Perhaps owing to mediocre translation, a few rifle shots were fired at us, one of which slightly wounded a naval officer. Eventually one of the attached Intelligence people was sent in by folboat to explain our presence, and shortly before dawn some Italians mistakenly came out to guide the ML into port.

By daybreak our presence on the island was secure. The Italians were timid at first, but became more genial during the course of the day when they realized that they were to be treated as allies and not as defeated enemies. Honours were paid by us to the Italian flag and reciprocated by a general guard of honour when the White Ensign was hoisted on the Port Office roof. As a spectacle for the novice traveller I found the crescent-shaped Castelrosso waterfront, with neat white-painted houses and grey volcanic hills behind, stunning. Our reception from the few people still living there was heartwarming. Bottles of a liqueur which tasted like vintage port were produced. Now that we had arrived at last as liberators it was clear how much the bombastic Italians had ground down the poor long-suffering Greeks over the many years of unjust occupation of the Dodecanese.

When it became clear that by landing in Castelrosso port we had avoided a large field of Italian anti-personnel mines, there were cheers all round. The Yorkshire wag Stanley Laverett came up to me and said, 'Sir, now we all know why you were so seasick!' At this point there was a pause while we waited for news from Rhodes. As it was the most important island in the Dodecanese I hoped to sail straight there from Castelrosso. With Rhodes in our hands the whole strategic picture in the Eastern Mediterranean area would change in the Allies' favour. I was enjoying a gin and tonic with Walter Milner Barry in the Port Office when round the corner and into the harbour appeared at MTB flying the Italian flag, and on board I saw George Jellicoe. Two other men were with him, who got out when the boat tied up. They were Kesterton, Jellicoe's wireless operator, and Colonel Farnetza, Campioni's Chief of Staff. We went into an immediate meeting with Colonel Turnbull, the no-non-sense Commander of Raiding Forces Middle East, who had just arrived by seaplane from Cyprus. Revived by a large whisky and soda, Jellicoe gave us a vivid, step-by-step account of the trials and tribulations of his mission. He looked physically and mentally exhausted. Clearly, any idea of occupying Rhodes was out of the question. We needed some direction as to what to do next. Talking among ourselves, we felt we should bypass Rhodes, press on into the Aegean and occupy as many of the islands as possible before the Germans got there, starting with Cos, which had an airfield, and Leros, the Italian naval base and military headquarters. On 11 September we put these proposals to GHQ, Cairo, and had a good night's sleep.

The following morning, with GHQ approval, Colonel

Turnbull left for Simi to strengthen the Italians there, while Jellicoe and I headed north for Cosa on ML 249, with ten of my 'S' Detachment men. We had an uneventful night. It was calm and warm, and sleeping on deck is always invigorating. A spectacular dawn found us off the south coast of Cos with the sun catching the hills as we rounded the eastern promontory facing the coast of Turkey, with more mountains, wooded and wild, away to starboard. From the south Cos appeared barren and austere. Approaching the town, houses and vineyards appeared, glittering in the strengthening sun. We did not know how we would be received, or if the Germans had forestalled us, or what the Italian garrison would feel about our sudden arrival. But as we neared the harbour I could see lots of children looking at us, and as we ran through the narrow entrance a crowd was waiting for us on the quay. The enthusiasm and joy of the inhabitants was touching in its spontaneity. Grapes were showered by the Greeks on our patrols as they went ashore. The Italian response to the Allied arrival was more muted, perhaps inflamed by rumours of recent events on Rhodes. But the Garrison Commander and his staff were co-operative. By noon most of the SBS men were occupying billets around Antimachia airfield in the centre of the island, and the officers sitting down to lunch in the mess. I remember a large meal of spectacular tagliatelle verde and red wine and exchanging 'so far so good' glances with Milner Barry across the crowded table. Meanwhile, back in the town of Cos, free haircuts and shaves were pressed upon us and 2nd Lieutenant Stefan Casulli, an Alexandrian who had joined the Greek Army and volunteered to serve with us, was borne shoulder-high to the square and entreated to make a speech.

After lunch Jellicoe left for Leros in an Italian MTB to discover the attitude and intentions of the Governor, Admiral Mascherpa, and if these proved amicable, to investigate the defences of the island and find a suitable area in which to drop supplies and reinforcements. The Admiral was co-operative, but our energies brought about an unexpectedly rapid reaction from Cyprus and Cairo.

On the afternoon of 13 September a Dakota aircraft, attended by a flight of South African Spitfires, arrived at Antimachia airfield. Just before midnight I helped guide down a company of the 11th Parachute Battalion on to the salt pans along the northern coast near Marmeti. Moreover, officialdom had given the increasingly mixed force operating in the Aegean a number, Force 292.

Cairo then announced that a General had been appointed to command it, who would shortly arrive on Cos. On my way back from the 11th Parachute drop there was a message that General Anderson wanted to see me. He was obviously pleased with the operational progress and asked me where I wanted to go next. I replied that Samos would suit me well, not least as the wine was good. This caused the General no difficulty and was operationally good news for me. How pleasant it was to be trusted by someone so senior, I reflected as I withdrew. I had never met a Lieutenant-General before!

After a most uneventful overnight passage the ML arrived at Samos. The second largest island in the Dodecanese has a skyline of rugged hills and almost touches Turkey. Our approach from the south through the narrows dominated by the wooded Turkish coastline into the port of Vathi was dramatic. Tying up in the harbour, the ML Captain reported to the Harbour Master. It became clear that the Samos garrison was a Blackshirt battalion of 1,500, who took a poor view of the arrival of a British military group of twenty-five! We felt it would be wise to accept their invitation for lunch. As I was walking along the harbour wall a stunning-looking dark-haired girl with a figure to match appeared with an unusual offer, 'Would you like a shave? I have kept my best razor for you' she purred! Life is full of the unexpected! Never one to refuse a good offer, I allowed this dazzling beauty to lead me by the hand to the cool of her barber's chair from which the rippling harbour water could be seen.

There are some events and moments which are frozen in one's mind. It was her deftness with the razor, the softness and purpose of her touch and the occasion itself which made it magical. Also, I wanted to look my best at our forthcoming lunch with the formidable-looking Island Commander.

Six officers had accepted the Island Commander's invitation to lunch, Milner Barry, the Commander and two officers from the ML, our seasoned and patient interpreter and myself. I had just been promoted to Major to give our tiny bluffing force a little more visible clout! The garrison officers' mess was a low stone building set in a fold in the wooded hills looking out to sea. We were met by a group of worried-looking young officers and ushered inside. There we were confronted by one of the most enormous men I have ever seen. I realized that this must be Primo Carnera, the Italian heavyweight boxing champion. Carnera was a bit slow on his feet, but as an in-fighter devastating! After lunch of minestrone, tagliatelle, veal, local cheese and fruit and two good wines, he began to unbend a bit. The armistice and our arrival were unforeseen. He saw his whole life and future military career on the line. He said he did not know what was going to happen next. I told him that soon we were being replaced by an army infantry battalion. He looked anxious, deflated, and at that point I thanked him and his officers for their hospitality and we left.

A couple of days later I was sitting having a drink in the harbour. A tall, slightly-built man approached and introduced himself as Michael Parish from Turkey. He was a member of a family of Levantine traders and knew all about what the SBS was doing in the Aegean. We started talking, and by the direction and extent of his contacts and knowledge it became apparent that he was working for MI9, an important organization for us during the war because it set up and funded agents, particularly in neutral countries, to help prisoners of war on the run, the so-called 'rat lines'. Several SBS captured in the Aegean escaped, got to Turkey and soon back to the unit. The most incredible 'rat line' story of all was that of George Tsoucas, captured in Rhodes on ANGLO, back through Switzerland, France, Spain and Gibraltar – a very tough and seriously determined character.

Parish told me that he was going to the island of Icaria in an Italian speed boat to sort out a problem between the Greek guerrillas and the Black Shirt garrison. During the voyage the boat's crew mutinied, having heard a radio news report from Rome that their hero Mussolini had been rescued by the daring German, Otto Skorzeny. To them Badoglio was a traitor. The crew suddenly produced weapons, there was a sharp gun-fight and Parish was wounded in the stomach. First landed at the island of Syros, then flown to Athens, he underwent surgery by the Germans, followed by interrogation in Belgrade. He was a prisoner for the rest of the war and survived. His book *Aegean Adventures 1940–43* is interesting stuff.

It was not long before a battalion of the Royal West Kent Regiment relieved us. We sailed to Kalymnos, a volcanic, treeless island immediately south of Leros. Kalymnos had long been the centre of the Dodecanese sponge-fishing fleet and we were billetted in a sponge warehouse. The factory and most of the island was owned by Mme Vouvalis, 'The Sponge Queen', a lady of great distinction. She gave a memorable dinner for Milner Barry, Stefan Casulli and myself, with delicious sea food. She was so exhilarated by the occasion that she led us into her garden and gave us spades to dig up bottles of the most delicious wine, concealed by her for years from the Italians.

On 1 October, 1943, it was decided that Kalymnos would make an ideal base for all raiding forces in the area, the SBS and the newly arrived and retrained LRDG, with Colonel Turnbull and Raiding Forces HQ in Leros. We looked upon Rhodes as our next target. The future looked bright, too bright for us to take seriously the warning that an enemy convoy had been observed sailing south-east from Naxos.

Bound for Rhodes was the general opinion. I returned to Kalymnos in an Italian MAAS boat with Jellicoe, Lieutenant Commander Ramseyer and Milner Barry, and after a memorable fish supper in a Greek restaurant we went to sleep full of plans for the future. However, we had neglected to take into account some of the wider issues of German policy in the Eastern Mediterranean and the Balkans.

There is little doubt that the announcement of the Italian armistice had surprised the German Balkan Command in Salonika just as much as it had the British GHQ in Cairo, and if the latter did have a few extra hours' notice, the former had the enormous advantage of efficient military formations already deployed throughout the Aegean. Moreover, the commanders of those formations had not long to wait for clear directions, for Hitler, faced with a threat to an area which provided him not only with bauxite, copper and chrome, but also protection from Allied bomber attack on the Ploesti oilfields, hardly hesitated for a moment. The whole Aegean area, and especially the Dodecanese would be held, he proclaimed, either by a continuation of co-operation between the Italian and German troops in the area, or, if the Italians showed signs of obeying the orders of the renegade Badoglio government, then by German forces alone, who would not hesitate to take and exert command. Within hours German officers were interviewing their nearest Italian counterparts in the islands and requesting specific assurances of loyalty from them.

It is impossible not to feel some sympathy for the Italian garrison commanders. Most of them were middle-aged, even elderly, senior officers whose service careers had been rewarded during recent years by appointments to these pleasant islands, where danger had been minimal, supplies from the homeland regular and of good quality, and duties easy enough hardly to disturb the even tenor of what resembled a happy retirement.

Suddenly they were faced with real danger and the necessity to make hard choices. Many of them, given the chance, would have been only too ready to welcome the British, for whom they felt regard and indeed some affection, in place of the Germans for whom they felt only respect tinged with fear, but few of them knew for certain the attitudes of their subordinates (Samos was not the only island which held a contingent of Blackshirts), and for many of them there were even more urgent reasons to temporize. The British and American armies might be ashore on the foot of Italy, but their own wives and families lived far away up in the north in such places as Bologna or Milan – and how long would the Allies take to get there?

Even more urgently, how long would it take the Allies, in this case the British alone, to arrive in these islands in sufficient strength to beat off not only the German forces already present with their abundant transport, excellent weapons and efficient organization, but also the reinforcements which would undoubtedly arrive from Greece should German control of the area appear in doubt? Admiral Campioni's actions might in the eyes of history appear equivocal and pusillanimous compared with those of some of his compatriots, say in Cos or Leros, but how great a distance separated them, when the choice had to be made, from the nearest German military formation?

This was the main consideration which affected control of the Aegean immediately following the Italian armistice. Those islands which previously had held only an Italian garrison – Cos, Leros, Samos, Simi, Stampalia, Icaria – fell easily under British influence once they had been visited by men of the SBS. Significantly, however, Crete and Rhodes remained firmly in the Axis camp and under German control. And once the situation stabilized and the battle-lines could be drawn Admiral Fricke in Athens and General Klemann on Rhodes could see quite clearly that they held the strongest cards and that if they played them well they could win the whole pack.

The first essential for them was to secure control of the air above the Aegean by occupying every island which contained a practicable airstrip. Extra Me 109 fighters and Ju 87 dive-bombers had quickly been flown into Maritsa and Calatos, and on 17 September the Ju's had begun a programme of attack on the nearest of the airstrips, Antimachia, on Cos. Cos by this time had already received substantial Allied reinforcement – more South African Spitfires, more ground crew, a large contingent of the RAF regiment, and a battalion of the Durham Light Infantry as main garrison troops. These last had spent months in Malta and thus knew all about shelter from air raids, and if their spirits were somewhat cast down by so rapid a reappearance of the sights and sounds of siege warfare, they nevertheless set about propping up damaged buildings with dour goodwill and efficiency, and helping the RAF ground staff to fill in craters.

Their presence had also allowed the withdrawal of the paratroop company to Cyprus, and of the SBS, some of whom had gone back to Castelrosso, while the bulk had gone to Kalymnos in preparation for a series of raids on German-held islands, especially, as had been mentioned, the one on Rhodes.

But that enemy convoy mentioned earlier had not, as we had thought, been 'Bound for Rhodes' at all. It had been bound for Cos, and it constituted the transport for *Kampfgrüppe Mueller*.

At 2am on the morning of 3 October I was woken up by the sound of heavy fighting on Cos. My heart sank. This was the last thing we had expected. As soon as it was light, I could see with binoculars an enemy assault force disembarking on the north coast, hiding between the towns of Cos and Antimachia. This was a battalion of the 65th Panzer Grenadier Regiment, tasked to drive across the neck of the island and meet the 16th Panzer Grenadiers, who had been landed near Cape Foca. Then German *Fallschirmjäger* from the Brandenburg Regiment dropped around Antimachia, heavy

Stuka attacks blew apart the defence posts, Me 109s shot up the Spitfires while they were still on the ground or taking off and chased away the Beaufighters which came across from Cyprus in an effort to bring succour to the hard-pressed defenders.

These by the evening had almost all been overwhelmed by *Kampfgrüppe Mueller* in a series of brilliant but violent actions, and by midnight the Germans controlled all of Cos except the dock area, upon which they focused searchlights and sniped and bombed everything that moved. Small parties of British and Italian soldiers sneaked their way out of town to climb the hills and make for a rendezvous at Cardamena with the admirable intention of carrying out their last orders, which were to try to continue the fight in guerrilla fashion, but most of them were to be rounded up after a very short time.

Meanwhile, all day long Milner Barry and the men of the SBS on Kalymnos had been horrified spectators of the battle: the silencing of one defensive position after another, the continuous arrival by sea of German reinforcements, and the unending flights of Luftwaffe aircraft overhead, all virtually uninterrupted. During the morning we had prepared ourselves and our weapons to undertake some form of interference in the onslaught taking place only a mile away across the water, but by the time orders arrived for us to land and aid the defenders of Antimachia it was quite obvious that it was already too late, and against the heavy weapons of the Panzer Grenadiers the small arms of a raiding force would in any case have been inadequate.

It seemed to Raiding Forces HQ on Leros and ourselves on Kalymnos that we should at once try to get as many British military out of Cos as we could. This tricky task fell to 'S' Detachment. Luckily, at that time in Kalymnos Harbour LS2 lay at anchor – Levant Schooner number two, commanded by Lieutenant McLeod, RNVR. The Levant Schooner Flotilla was one of the great imaginative ideas of the war in the Eastern Mediterranean. I don't know who thought this up but I suspect the transglobe navigator Lieutenant Adrian Seligman, RNR. A typical LSF caique was of local appearance and construction, very seaworthy, about 15 tons. It had been specially modified in Beirut with a powerful, silent-running diesel engine installed, an easily collapsible mast and camouflage nets and bamboo poles to break the outline of the vessel when lying up by day. A radio linked it to its base at Beirut. LSF was the naval equivalent of the SBS, manned by highly skilled and motivated volunteers with a taste for danger and the unorthodox. Needless to say, we got on very well together.

At about 3 pm on 3 October with the continuous noise of the battle of Cos 'just over the water', I talked to Milner Barry, Stefan Casulli and Alec McLeod about their task on Cos. We sat uneasily in the shade with the calm water of Kalymnos Harbour rippling in the afternoon sunlight. I had an ancient Italian map of Cos, McLeod some naval charts. My orders from Raiding Force HQ (RFHQ) in Leros were to land that night to support the garrison at Antimachia and help people to escape, keeping RFHQ informed by radio. We discussed the size of the SBS group under Captain Milner Barry and agreed that Casulli and twelve men, including three signallers, be transported by Lieutenant McLeod in LS2. They were in good hands; Alec McLeod was one of the LSF stars.

When the more violent sounds of battle had died down and only the occasional crack of a rifle shot pierced the night, I watched Milner Barry and his patrol put to sea aboard LS2. They crept around the eastern end of Cos and went ashore on the south coast in a small bay where they immediately ran into a party of RAF men from Antimachia, who told them in detail of the events of the day. After sending the RAF men away in the caique and arranging for its return on the night of the 7th/8th, Milner Barry and his men found a small wadi a little way inland and took up residence there, the rest of that night and the early hours of the morning being spent bringing up from the beach the rest of their own gear, the wireless set and its infernal batteries.

During the following day watch was kept from a high point at the end of the wadi and a dozen assorted army and RAF men were found and brought in. Then at dusk German infantry were seen approaching in line, driving Italian troops in front, and soon the wadi was full of 'hysterical Italians who attached themselves to us, and the Germans began to mortar the wadi at both ends.'

Altogether, over three days and by parking some escapers temporarily in the nearby islands of Nisiros and others in Turkey, McLeod's crew and Milner Barry's patrol rescued sixteen British officers and seventy-four NCOs and men, together with a very large number of Italians and a few brave Greeks. It had been a nerve-racking operation, and at the end of it Milner Barry was flown back to Alexandria to go into hospital suffering from exhaustion and a bad case of desert sores, while the rest of his patrol went to Castelrosso, for Kalymnos and the 'Sponge Queen' had been reluctantly abandoned to the Germans.

For his indomitable part in this successful and hazardous operation I recommended that Milner Barry be Mentioned in Despatches, which, I am pleased to say, he was.

Gratified by their success on Cos, the Germans then turned their attention to the next most important island still in British hands: Leros, with its naval port and fortress, long proclaimed by the Italians to be the crucial base from which naval command of approaches to Salonika and the Dardanelles could be exercised.

During October Leros was heavily reinforced by three infantry battalions from Malta. When challenged by Whitehall as to what was going on, General Wilson and GHQ Cairo maintained that it would now be very difficult to bring them back, that keeping them there, given Turkish aid, was possible and would oblige the Germans to retain forces in the Aegean which might be used elsewhere. What Cairo failed to appreciate was that command of the air is vital for all military or naval movements, and even more essential for the defence of isolated positions. Why the C-in-C thought 'Turkish aid' would suddenly become available to protect British troops from the threat of destruction is unclear. The Royal Navy was the first to feel the shock of German reaction. A large number of destroyers and cruisers were sent to Leros carrying troops and supplies. I remember watching in horror from Leros while an endless stream of dive bombers attacked a destroyer near the island of Levitha, some thirty miles away, and eventually sank it.

Leros is eight miles long and four wide, with two narrow mile-long beaches in the middle. There are three barren, hilly features each about 1,000 feet high. In the south-west corner is the all-weather harbour Portolago Bay. The island outline resembles a large cowpat trodden on by two feet! There is no airfield. Turkey is about thirty miles away. I moved to Leros from Kalymnos with 'S' Detachment around 15 October. We found ourselves part of the garrison defence force manning road blocks at night and in danger by day because the Stuka attacks occurred every morning with monotonous regularity. For me and for all the SBS this was a terrifying and demoralizing experience. RFHQ was in some buildings beside the water in Portolago Bay. One evening I was summoned to a meeting there. I did not notice a destroyer refuelling nearby. Suddenly out of the blue came the familiar shrieking sound of a Stuka on to its target. I threw myself full length, hugging the ground. The bomb landed 50 metres away with a massive explosion. A brave man standing up firing a machine gun completely disappeared. The blast lifted me up and down like a sack of potatoes. From the top of my head to my boots I was covered in fine white dust, as if I had been working in a flour mill. I got up badly shaken, looking like a ghost and partially deaf and remember David Lloyd Owen (LRDG) appearing to comfort me and saying, 'David,

you look terrible. You should go away for some days' rest.'
I took this good advice and left for Samos on an Italian water
boat next day.

Antonio, the waterboat Captain, was a real Dodecanese
character. His job was to load the boat with Leros water, sail
slowly north to deliver it to a cluster of waterless islands,
refill in Samos and repeat the process heading south. Clearly
he had cornered the water market because he looked at ease
with the world and prosperous. His mate was a remarkable
cook. I remember a fine green tagliatelli with a delicate
crayfish sauce. As you can imagine, with this kind of treatment it did not take me long to recover and return to the
dreaded Leros.

For me at that time Leros was an advanced form of hell.
There were deep lines of exhaustion and defeat on all our
faces, and the whiff of disaster lying just ahead. We were all
demoralized by the ceaseless bombing and the fact that the
enemy called all the shots. It was like Dunkirk and Tobruk
all over again. I longed to get away.

Amid this Stygian gloom a shaft of light suddenly appeared
which I remember to this day. For much of my time in the
SBS I had the good fortune to have a first-class personal
signaller in the shape of John Wilkinson. He was training to
be a solicitor when the war began and he joined the Royal
Corps of Signals. We were lying around uneasily under some
olive trees during one of the rare moments when no enemy
aircraft were overhead when I saw John Wilkinson in the
distance waving a piece of paper and at the same time
indicating silence by putting a finger over his lips. Curious, I
walked over. He handed me a written message from RFHQ
that Anders Lassen had been awarded a third Military Cross
for extraordinary gallantry during the battle of Simi in
September. Lassen had been attached to Ian Lapraik and 'M'
Detachment for the Simi operation, but was now back with
'S' Detachment on Leros. I took Wilkinson aside and said,
'Look, this award is so exceptional that I want to give him

the medal ribbon personally. Let us make all the preparations without him knowing. We can then have a gigantic celebration.' And so it was. Wilkinson was neat-fingered. In no time he had produced an accurate replica of the Military Cross ribbon, using white paper and gentian blue dye, to which two rosettes cut from the silver foil found in every cigarette packet were attached. Later that evening I asked all the 'S' Detachment people of Leros to assemble 'for an interesting event'. About fifteen were there, including Digger Rice, the Australian, Hancock, Cree, some of the Irish patrol and of course Lassen. I said, 'We can forget our Leros woes because I have just had a message from RFHQ that Anders Lassen has been awarded his third Military Cross for gallantry on Simi, and I am going to pin the ribbon on his chest now.' The roar of approval echoed around the bare hills above as I walked forward to shake his hand. Our eyes met: for once in his life he was nonplussed and mumbled an incoherent reply. But, knowing him so well, I knew how touched and proud he was and we of him. We drank everything in sight long into the night and slept like babes.

On 11 November an anxious George Jellicoe came up to me and said, 'We know the Germans are going to attack Leros tomorrow. There is no point in both of us being here. I suggest you leave tonight for Turkey.' This was the best news I had had for a long time. I found a small caique in Pandeli Bay on the east coast of Leros ready to go to Gumushuk. With me were Captain Chevalier, Lieutenant Casulli and eight SBS men. We left about midnight. The caique's engine was old and spewed out a trail of sparks. I told the skipper to put a bucket over the exhaust to kill the give-away sparks. Just as well I did, because we missed the *Kampfgrüppe Mueller* and the Leros invasion fleet by less than a mile.

Dawn found us at Gumushuk, a small Turkish fishing village. Just out to sea and so close one could almost touch it in the morning sun was a German destroyer defiantly flying an enormous swastika on its stern. Meanwhile, on Leros the battle we had all dreaded rumbled on and became increasingly intense as more enemy troops and aircraft became involved. After five days of bitter fighting, with heavy casualties on both sides, in the afternoon of 16 November the embattled Commander, Brigadier Tilney, surrendered. Of the four infantry battalions who had fought on Leros during the period of the campaign, less than 250 survivors got away. One third of the Mediterranean Fleet was lost. With some pre-planning and some luck, George Jellicoe got more than twenty SBS and others out with him in a caique from Pandeli Bay in the west of Leros.

Thus a disastrous campaign for the British ended in abject defeat. For us in the SBS there were both lessons and opportunities. Luckily, we had few casualties because we were not heavily involved.

I came away from that ugly period with the clear impression that the Germans in the Aegean were well-trained, versatile soldiers; we must be the same. German deployment on the islands, however, would provide challenging raiding opportunities for us.

It was impossible for Raiding Forces to operate during the Aegean winter because of bad weather. We spent the period November, 1943, to February, 1944, resting, ski-ing in the Lebanese mountains for a change of scene and preparing for the operations in the Aegean that lay ahead. At that time Raiding Forces Middle East consisted of the HQ at Azzib on the Palestine coast north of Haifa and four operational units. These were The Heros Lokos (the Greek Sacred Squadron) formed originally in the Spartan Wars of 300 BC and revived whenever the Greek nation faced a military crisis, SBS, LRDG and Levant Schooner Flotilla, in all totalling some 650 experienced and intrepid characters. I suppose the most remarkable leader of all in those far distant times was Colonel Tsigantes commanding the Sacred Squadron. Dark and short, with a deeply lined face hidden behind sun-glasses, he looked like a prosperous restaurateur. But he was highly sophisticated and charming, spoke five languages and was fearless in action. Above all, he had the wisdom and experience of a man born in my father's generation.

For some reason, I believe bad luck, and because more of them were there, the LRDG had heavy casualties in the Aegean campaign. Guy Prendergast, their commander, got away from Leros, but the rising star, Jake Eason Smith, was killed by a sniper there. Many others, including John Oliver, were forced to surrender when they ran out of ammunition after four days of bitter fighting. They had to recruit, train and reorganize. They reappeared the following year in the Adriatic under the able leadership of David Lloyd Owen.

The Raiding Force Middle East raids in the Aegean began in the middle of January, 1944. These raids were, of course, part and parcel of a much larger campaign, though of this the participants were not all fully aware. Operation Overlord, the cross-Channel invasion, was to take place in five months' time and a great deal of Britain's Mediterranean strategy was aimed at reducing the strength of the German forces concentrated in Northern France to meet it. On paper it would mean that the contribution to be made by a raiding force of around 400 men from the Greek Sacred Squadrom and SBS would, in the opinion of Middle East HQ, with help from the SBS and Royal Navy, achieve unexpected results through a confident campaign. For this purpose the Aegean was divided: north of Leros, Greek Sacred Squadron: south of Leros, SBS. It was at this point that we began to use large, 100-ton plus, caiques hidden deep in the innumerable inlets in neutral Turkish waters as secure bases from which to plan and mount our raids.

The first stage of this campaign involved the destruction of as much German-controlled shipping as possible, hence the SBS concentration on the wrecking of caiques and harbour installations; hence also the transmission every night of information regarding German maritime activity to Cairo for the further attention of the RAF and the Royal Navy. These measures, it was reckoned, would produce two results: the SBS attacks themselves would bring about the strengthening of each island's German garrison, while the destruction of the shipping would ensure the retention of those over-strength garrisons on comparatively unimportant islands.

Once on the islands, in fact, the Germans would be unable to get off, and, as time went by, the SBS net would be cast ever wider until even the far-flung islands in the western Cyclades or the northern Sporades would be under threat, and the enemy forced to inject more and more troops into ever more inaccessible defences. Throughout the first six months of 1944 this campaign was increased, indeed, intensified.

There were three SBS Detachments involved and we arranged for them to be changed every six weeks. At the end of March, 1944, the periodic changeover was due and 'S' Detachment took over from 'L' Detachment. At the time I was quite ill in the Italian hospital at Haifa, with the bane of military life in the Middle East at that time, jaundice. Snoozing quietly one afternoon, suddenly a dark-haired figure in crisp khaki uniform appeared silently at the foot of my bed. A stern, commanding voice penetrated deep into my subconscious. It was George Jellicoe. 'David, what on earth are you doing here? You should be in the Aegean with your men.' 'I am quite ill, George, and I like looking at the pretty Italian nurses.' 'I know you do; so would I. Come and join us soon!'. And with that he turned on his heel and left. George Jellicoe had then, and has to this day, the strength and constitution of an ox!

I felt excited, interested and a bit apprehensive as to how my task would develop when I first saw the RN ship *Tewfiq* moored deep in the wooded inlet Yeti Atdullah. The familiar, friendly faces of Milner Barry, Lassen, Casulli, Nicholson, Conby, Darcy, Henderson and others crowded around the ship's rails asking if I had mail from home or newspapers. I had both. Climbing aboard *Tewfiq*, in which I was to spend the next six weeks, I was reminded of some piratical scene from *Treasure Island*, with contemporary arms, ammunition, equipment and noises for good measure. There was the homely smell of unwashed bodies, mixed with a whiff of garlic cooking in the galley. The quiet background noise of the ship's activities was overlaid by the raucous din from the petrol-driven patrol radio battery-chargers. The ship's large hold was filled with masses of men sleeping in hammocks and bunks. Forward of the hold was a large office used as an operation planning room, table in the middle, chairs around, walls covered with maps. There, too, was the terminal of our radio link with RFHQ at Azzib, and the outside world. I pinched for myself a small panelled cabin with a comfortable bunk and fitted writing desk. It was two flights of steep, wooden stairs above the Ops Room. I insisted on having all the bits and pieces one needs for SBS operational planning such as maps, operational files, air photographs, moon charts, typewriters, magnifying glasses, pens, etc, to hand. The good Milner Barry had done this.

The first thing I had to do after arrival was chat with Milner Barry about how things were going. I remember him sitting in the shade under the ship's open awning, whisky and soda in hand, his brown face turned towards me. During January and February the weather had been appalling, with non-stop northerly gales. Accordingly, 'L' Detachment's operations were confined to the Dodecanese. I wished to attack targets further to the west but bad weather still intervened. This gave me time to get to know some newcomers to the Detachment and reinforce old friendships. An unusual character was John Lodwick, whom George Jellicoe had sent up to join me. Speaking fluent French, he had joined the Foreign Legion on the outbreak of war and had been taken prisoner with them in France in 1940. Lodwick had been the only Englishman in a prison camp in France when the Royal Navy shelled and sank the French squadrons at

Mers el Kebir, and only the loyalty of fellow Légionnaires had saved him from degradation and probably mutilation at the hands of the other prisoners, egged on by the amused German guards. Later the Legion engineered his escape through Spain, and his subsequent adventures before joining the SBS had included another brief spell in both France and Spain as an SOE agent.

He had come to SBS via the Commando Training School at Achnacarry. He was small and dark, and now and then wore the Croix de Guerre ribbon. Lieutenant Kingsley Clarke had the look of a prosperous farmer. Indeed his family had farmed the rich soil beside the Thames below Windsor Castle for generations. Lieutenant Keith Balsillie was South African. It gave me a real sense of purpose and satisfaction to chat with them about future operations. Also, it was comforting to have on board all the Operation ALBUMEN team and also Stefan Casulli, who had just heard that his Belgian wife Yvette was expecting a baby in Alexandria. We raised a hopeful cheer and drank a monumental toast when this good news ran round the ship. Little did we know that this marvellous man would never see his child. He died in action on the island of Thira in a highly successful raid led by Anders Lassen on 22 April, 1944.

As we had surprise, the initiative and good men involved, I planned each raid with great care. Sitting round the Operations Room table with maps, up-to-date air photographs and latest intelligence reports on enemy activity were the Patrol Commander and his senior NCO, the LSF caique commander and his coxswain, Nick Morris, the clerk taking notes, and myself. We covered in great detail the object and method of the raid and how the group were going to get there and back. This was confirmed in a written Operation Order typed out by Morris and signed by me, to the Patrol Commander, copied to each caique commander at HQ Raiding Force Middle East. My operational philosophy, as everyone knew, was to avoid getting into a hopeless corner.

Better by far to get back safely, ready for the next operation. In truth we could only operate successfully on moonless nights.

The first raid was against shipping and opportunity targets on Stampalia by Lodwick's patrol on 26 March. Bad weather dogged the operation, but they took the German naval commander of the island prisoner with his guest that night at dinner, a captain in the German merchant marine, and then shot up a German billet and wounded most of its inhabitants. However, attempts to reach ships in the small harbour were unsuccessful and the following night, perhaps slightly conscience-stricken, the ML returned early to take them off after a comparatively unprofitable operation.

The Cyclades were as yet untouched but habitable staging places had to be found for Harbour Defence Motor Launches (HDMLs) and caiques before COMARO 1, the Royal Naval Operational Planners, would agree to send their craft out. I sent a reconnaissance party to the island of Kevagos. It returned on 3 April with a favourable report.

Meanwhile, two successful operations took place. Clarke's patrol captured nine Italians on Patmos and a small caique was captured on Msino and taken back to base. A co-ordinated attack on enemy radar stations was asked for by GHQ. The radar on the island of Scarpanto was the target given to 'S' Detachment. As Scarpanto is midway between Rhodes and Crete I decided that the Patrol under Captain Blyth should stage at the island of Alimnia, which is just off Rhodes. They left Bira on 5 April, 1944, aboard LS24 and were never seen again. The patrol contained a group of SBS stars. As soon as I had written 'overdue' on my Patrol Board I had the gut feeling that something terrible had happened to them. It had. They were the ill-fated Alimnia Patrol, the subject of a chapter later on. Discussing this highly unusual, almost inexplicable loss with Milner Barry, Lassen and others, we came to the conclusion that the Patrol must have been betrayed in some way. I sent a full report on these lines to RFHQ. On 9 April I was ordered temporarily to stop all operations east of the line Lapia-Piscopi because of the probable capture of LS24. On 15 April the base was moved to Baisu Bay.

On 16 April the operational ban was lifted and we were able to carry out a number of successful raids in the Cyclades, as well as keeping pressure on the Dodecanese. My plan was to attack Mykonos, Ios and Thira simultaneously, priority targets to be shipping and communications. On 19 April Lassen's and Balsillie's patrols sailed for Thira under Lassen's command. I remember studying in great detail maps and air photographs of the extinct volcanic crater with Lassen, Balsillie and the caique commander, to see if a caique could be concealed under camouflage nets during the day, preferably under the enemy's nose. We believed it could. As LSI and AII sailed for Thira I took a snap of Lassen on the stern, puffing away at a cigarette, with his men all around. It is probably the best photograph ever taken of him. At dawn next morning they arrived at Sirina, an uninhabited island we often used as a staging point. The next night they stopped at another uninhabited island, Anidhros, and from there sailed for Thira, where they arrived after dark. Lassen went ashore with Casulli to collect information from the islanders.

During the following day information was gathered and plans laid. Three attacks would be mounted, the first by Keith Balsillie and his men, who would climb to the highest point of the island and destroy the W/T station and its outpost near the village of Meravigli; the second would be made by Sergeant Henderson on his own, his task to attack and capture or kill the German commander, *Leutnant* Hesse, and his orderly in the house sequestered for their use. Lassen himself would lead the rest of the men against the main billet, which was reputed to hold thirty-eight Italians and ten Germans.

'This report was partly false,' Lassen wrote afterwards, with a distinct note of disappointment. 'There were less than thirty-five men in the billet. We succeeded in getting the main force into the billet unobserved, in spite of barking dogs and sentries. The living quarters comprised twelve rooms ... it was our intention to take the troops there prisoner. This idea had to be abandoned, and will have to be abandoned in the future, until raiding parties are issued with good torches.'

In default of the torches, a systematic but ruthless policy was followed, Sergeant Nicholson kicking open the door of a room, Lassen throwing in two grenades, Nicholson then raking the room, especially the corners, with Bren-gun fire, after which Lassen would go in and finish everything off with his pistol. Incredibly, those two came out unscathed, but Stefan Casulli, following the same practice but standing *in* the doorway instead of to one side of it, received a burst through his chest and died almost instantly, while outside the billet Sergeant Kingston caught a bullet in the stomach.

Marines Trafford and Harris were also slightly wounded outside the billet when a German patrol and some of the sentries opened fire, but at that moment two things happened to distract both danger and attention from them. First, a fear-crazed Italian jumped from an upper window, and as the billet was in fact the office of the local branch of the Bank of Athens he had a forty-foot drop to endure; then Sergeant Nicholson emerged from the main doorway and dispersed the enemy with his Bren gun, firing from the hip.

In the meantime Keith Balsillie had reached Meravigli in good time but had found the lay-out of the outpost and W/T station not as expected. The posts were all, in fact, contained in three neighbouring houses, so, after stationing Corporal Hughes and Bombardier Fowler in covering positions with their Brens, Balsillie and the others quietly entered the first. In it they found a man asleep in bed, whom Kahane gently awoke.

'For you, my friend, the war is over,' Kahane informed him in German. 'Now be a good fellow, get dressed and take us to your comrades. But first tell us where the wireless set is.'

Undoubtedly impressed by the considerable firepower in the hands of Kahane's associates, but unable completely to throw off the bonds of discipline, the man led the party to the next house and almost formally introduced them to his *Unteroffizier*, who himself, convinced by the logic of the Tommy guns, took them back to the first house where they found not only the W/T but also three more Germans in bed, apparently too deeply asleep to have heard the previous entry.

The W/T was prepared for demolition, three more Germans were collected from yet another house, and in due course Balsillie, his corporals and his men together with their eight prisoners, made their way back towards their rendezvous with Lassen, which they reached about 0330. As they trotted back down the first slope they were cheered by the sounds of the W/T installation being blown to pieces.

Sergeant Henderson had not been quite as successful as the others, for not only did the lay-out of his target differ from what had been deduced from the information to hand, but his quarry did not react in the expected fashion. Working on the assumption that, at the sounds of battle, the German Commandant would at least send someone to find out what was happening even if he did not emerge himself, Henderson stationed himself in the shadows of the front garden by the door. But when the crash and rattle of Lassen's attack came echoing up towards the house, there was no apparent reaction at all. Puzzled, Henderson threw a grenade which blew out a window, and then a second which went through and exploded in the front room, but not until he was actually climbing through the shattered frame did he hear any sounds of occupation – a murmur of voices from the rear which prompted him to drop back into the garden and double smartly around to the back garden gate.

But he was too late, for as he raced around the corner he

heard other footsteps in an equal hurry fading rapidly away into the distance, increasing speed remarkably after the explosion of the grenade which the thoroughly frustrated Sergeant hurled after them. Lassen was not impressed by Henderson's report half an hour later; in fact, he was not much impressed by several facets of the actions which had taken place, as his 'notes' at the end of his own reports indicate:

'There is no doubt that shooting up barracks at night requires a great deal of skill and experience, such as only the older men in the SBS have, and which will not be found in reinforcements.

'Lack of experience must be made up by rigid training, especially in street and house fighting, and they should be generally taught how to look after themselves; not to stand in front of doors, for example. The standard of marching among the recruits was poor . . .

'As usual Sgt Nicholson, Cpl Sibbet and Cpl O'Reilly did extremely well, and were calm and efficient during the action.'

By 29 April Lassen, his men and his ships were all back at base.

On 22 April Lodwick's patrol went to Kalymnos, where he destroyed the cable station and blew up ten caiques in the main shipyard, including one excellently equipped craft belonging to the local Gestapo. At the same time Lodwick sent Sergeant Henderson and the American, Porter Jarrell, to attack a German billet, and for their pains they were chased over the hills for many miles, laden down with the weight of their Bren guns and ammunition.

Such aggressive behaviour was now becoming rather unusual for garrison troops in the Aegean. Other men sent by Lodwick to an isolated garrison fired shots at the billet door and even blew up nearby telegraph poles, but the soldiers inside stayed where they were, perhaps feeling humiliated by knowing quite well what their tormentors were hoping for and determined not to give it to them. In their situation, discretion was undoubtedly the better part of valour.

While this was going on, another newcomer, Lieutenant Kingsley Gordon Clarke, inevitably and invariably known as 'Nobby', had set out to repeat Bruce Mitford's tour of Patmos, Lipsos and Archi. He found Patmos garrisoned by ten Italians who preferred to surrender before a shot was fired than try conclusions with yet another SBS party, and the other two islands empty of both spoils and enemy.

The pace of island attacks now increased. Patrols were despatched as often and as quickly as transport became available for them, generally with specific tasks to carry out on each island – destruction of caiques and harbour facilities or telegraph and power stations; harassing of German garrisons; capture of Italians; reconnaissance for larger raids to be carried out in the future, or simply the gathering of reports on enemy shipping movements or regular air traffic. Always, however, the aim was to make their presence felt, to demonstrate that every harbour, every billet, every manned post was vulnerable to sudden attack.

As soon as Clarke was back from his three-island tour he was sent off to Amorgos, where he found only one German still on the island, in bed with his mistress at the time of discovery. Three men of his patrol were then detached to Nisiros and killed three Germans who discovered their whereabouts and attempted to catch them while they were still asleep in a cave; fortunately Corporal Holmes was a light sleeper and his Bren gun was beside him.

Nobby Clarke, now a captain, landed on Ios on the evening of 25 April, quickly to discover that the Germans garrisoning the island were occupying dispersed billets and apparently taking little precautions against such operations as he was about to launch. He therefore decided somewhat optimistically, to try to eliminate all opposition in the preliminary stage and thus be able to carry out his sabotage missions in peace and quiet. With this in mind, he, Corporal Pomford and an attached Civil Affairs Officer named McClelland broke into one of the billets during the late evening of the following day. Clarke and his men then sailed for Amorgos which they cleared of the entire German garrison of one officer and nine men.

Quite obviously, one of the strategic aims of these operations would soon be achieved and many more German troops would be sent out to reinforce the island garrisons. Equally obviously, this would take some little time to arrange, even given the German organizational talent – so I thought we might achieve even more successful lightning strikes while the opposition was still weak. Lassen could go out again almost immediately.

Perhaps German reaction time was a little under-estimated; perhaps more thought should have been given to reconnaissance, for when Lassen and his thirteen men arrived on the coast of Paros they found rows of pitched tents alongside a newly constructed airstrip, and although the occupants were workmen of the Todt construction organization and not soldiers as such, they nevertheless kept an excellent guard. Wisely, Lassen made no attempt to force penetration through so alert a screen and withdrew, but not before sending out Sergeant Nicholson on one lone mission and Parachutist Perkins, another fluent German speaker, on another.

Perkins surprised a German officer who unfortunately refused to accept his assurance that the war was over for him and had to be killed. Nicholson persuaded another German officer to accompany him peacefully (the officer was perhaps rendered more tractable by the fact that he was wearing nothing except a flowered dressing-gown). However a fight developed as they both left the house which Nicholson resolved with fragmentation grenades, killing his attackers as well as, unfortunately, his prisoner in the process. This caused Nicholson disquiet as the man had appeared friendly and well-disposed.

While Lassen was being frustrated at Paros, Nobby Clarke and I were preparing for more far-flung operations, and on 16 May Clarke and another newcomer to SBS, Captain Stobie, landed on Naxos with two patrols to make contact with a reputed guerrilla unit there. In this they were successful, so, despite the fact that the German garrison was not only alert as a result of the Paros raid but excellently dug-in around the most worthwhile target, Clarke decided to combine with the guerrillas and attack a small German billet in the town of Naxos itself, reputed to hold an officer and seventeen German soldiers.

The result was a pitched battle in which time was on the side of the defenders, but in the hour which was all Clarke would allow himself one of the two houses of which the billet consisted was completely demolished by plastic bombs, and a considerable weight of fire was poured into the second, from which, however, a strong resistance continued up to the moment Clarke gave the signal to withdraw. But he and his men were left undisturbed by the enemy for the next three days until transport arrived to take them home, with three men slightly wounded and one very weak from malaria.

This was the last main strike by 'S' Detachment. I felt a bit uneasy sitting safely and comfortably at base while sending everyone else to face great danger. So I descended on the island of Saphos during one balmy night, capturing a caique in the harbour there and one German soldier with an appalling cold!

Meanwhile Harold Chevalier ranged the waters to the north of Samos with a mixed fleet engaged upon pure piracy. Small craft he looted of anything obviously belonging to the enemy and then despatched them on their way with warnings of ever-increasing danger to German-chartered shipping; one large caique with its German crew he captured entire and brought it and its cargo of general stores, plus crew, back to base.

'S' Detachment operations carried out in the Aegean between 26 March and 9 June, 1944, resulted in :-

Caiques captured	3
sunk or damaged	12
Representing about	500 tons

W/T stations destroyed	3
captured	11
Cable, stations destroyed	3
Food landed	25 tons

Casualties – enemy

Germans killed	32	Italians killed	10
wounded	12	wounded	10
prisoner	23	prisoner	23
	67		43

Casualties – our troops

Killed	2
Wounded	3
Missing	5	– Alimnia Patrol

| *Landings* | 25 |
| Targets attacked | 17 |

After the climax of the raids of 22 April, perhaps these operations were less spectacular and less obviously worthwhile, but there were still the 'invisible' profits of effect upon enemy morale and, more importantly, upon enemy dispositions. By early May nearly 4,000 extra German troops had either arrived in the Aegean islands during the previous few weeks or were on their way there, and this was in addition to the six admittedly tired and under-strength divisions, resting from their ordeals on the Russian front, who had been there at the beginning of the period.

For this satisfactory development the Greek Sacred Squadron, SBS and LSF must take joint credit. Looking back over so many years serving with the SAS, it is 'S' Detachment's performance in the Aegean in 1944 which to this day fills me with deep admiration and pride. We had a key task to perform. The operations were well planned and carried out in a highly professional way at all levels. I reflected as we sailed quietly south back to Beirut how special these officers and men were. You could take them on SAS operations anywhere in the world and they would perform well. I was incredibly lucky to be leading them.

Once back at Athlit I held a debriefing of all the Detachment officers and men who had been in the Aegean, and those who had not. We felt we had been lucky to get away with so few casualties. Next time the Germans would be better prepared and more resolute as the war inexorably turned against them. We agreed that more training was needed in weapon-handling, use of ground, marching and load-carrying. There was fulsome praise for Clarke and Nicholson. I recommended the former for a Military Cross and the latter for the Distinguished Conduct Medal to add to the Military Medal he had gained on Operation ALBUMEN. These quickly came through. I remember sending for Nicholson and telling him. Typically he could not understand why he had been singled out. The celebratory feasting continued for several days and nights.

The armed forces, particularly the army, are great places for nicknames. They are both endearing and revealing. So it was in the SBS. Allott was called 'Tramp' because he dressed and ate like a tramp, and, it was said, smelt like one too! Lassen became, after the Thira raid, 'Andy the deadly Viking'. George Jellicoe inevitably was 'the Lord'. What the Lord said, you did. I became 'Dinky', cockney slang for 'neat and tidy'. Walter Milner Barry, because of his age, was 'Pop'. The Quarter-master Sergeant Jenkins of the Royal Marines, who could lay his hands on any piece of clothing and equipment long since unavailable, was 'the Soldiers' Friend'.

12

A Shipwreck and a
Turkish Bath

March, 1944

I claim the rare distinction of enduring, and surviving, a bona
fide shipwreck. It happened like this.

Without strong support and generous help from the neutral Turks, the Greek Sacred Squadron, the SBS and LSF
would have been unable to operate effectively against the
Germans in the Aegean north of Rhodes. The Turks provided two vital elements: secure anchorages hidden deep
in Turkish Territorial waters for our base ships and an
abundant supply of provisions – meat, vegetables, fruit,
water, etc – to augment our rigid military diet. The place we
used to get our supplies was the port of Bodrum, the ancient
Halicarnassus, the one city in the Levant Alexander the Great
failed to take.

A large number of Greek naval vessels were sunk or
otherwise put out of action at the time of the German
occupation of Greece in 1941. This put a number of experienced Greek Royal Naval officers high and dry without a
ship to command. Several joined LSF which offered action
against the enemy. One of these was the exuberant Commander Andrea Londos, RHN. I remember him coming up
to me and saying, 'David, I am just going to Bodrum to pick
up some supplies. Would you like to come with me?'
Longing for any opportunity to escape from base with this
amusing man, I agreed without hesitation. It was a night

passage with a slight swell from the south. I went to sleep, tucked away deep in the LSF's bowels.

The next happening would be better described by Joseph Conrad than by me. There was a sudden crack as the caique keeled over. I was ejected from my bunk. Sea water rushed in, accompanied by the deadly noise of ship's timbers grinding against rocks. Quickly struggling to the surface, I saw we had missed the harbour entrance by about 10 metres. Andrea Londos, who had retained his Commander's cap untouched, stood there swearing. Some Turkish soldiers with fixed bayonets then appeared on the harbour wall above us to find out what was going on. Clearly we were a highly suspicious lot, so the Turks marched us to Bodrum Castle and locked us up there while they checked on our credentials. It was a bitterly cold night and we were shivering from our dousing in the sea. A sympathetic Turkish soldier spotted my teeth chattering and lit a warming fire from branches lying around the castle floor. As more branches were thrown on and shadows flickered on the castle walls, some of the Turkish soldiers began their local dances with incredible stamps, gyrations and leaps, and we began to sing in unison. The tune the Turks liked best was 'Lloyd George knew my father'.

The amusing thing is that Lloyd George and my father really did know each other. In the latter part of the First War my father was Military Secretary to Field Marshal Haig in France and LG often appeared. My father thought him 'very tricky indeed'. LG's waspish comment about Haig, 'brilliant to the top of his boots,' fits.

There was a lull in this jovial campfire singing and I heard the sound of horses' hooves at full gallop on the road leading towards us. Silence – then the castle door was opened and a young Turkish officer with a large black cloak and a curved sword appeared to say that we were free to leave. It was then three in the morning.

I heard that Bodrum had one of the finest Hammams (hot baths) in the district. Feeling and looking scruffy, I went to have a look that day. On approaching the bath, which was outside the town, I saw an enormous, well-built Turk wearing a turban and eating tangerines from a large wicker basket. As I approached he rose from the shade of an acacia tree and barred my way. I went into a nearby café to discover I had chosen ladies' day! A pity, as some stunning-looking Turkish beauties appeared later! I returned next day to have one of the most refreshing baths ever, followed by delicious tangerines bought from the faithful, loyal eunuch!

13

Hitler's Commando Order and the Alimnia Patrol

April, 1944

Every now and then I have twinges of remorse about the fate of the Alimnia Patrol. Here is the story.

After Dunkirk there was a need for us to know how well defended the enemy coastline was. Also, we needed to develop the procedures and technique for landing on and getting off enemy-held coastline. A number of Commando Raids for this purpose took place in the summer of 1940 on the Channel Islands. On one raid two German soldiers were taken prisoner and shot in circumstances indicating they had been executed. This was reported to Hitler. He was furious. Soon afterwards, Hitler's Commando Order was issued. This written order to all subordinate commanders said that all captured Commandos should be interrogated in depth, tortured and shot.

We all knew about Hitler's Commando Order, but it did not stop us operating. We took great care never to be captured by the Germans. If this should happen, escape as soon as possible. We wore no unit insignia or badges of rank, only a personal identity disc round the neck.

In early April, 1944, there was an order from RFHQ that we should destroy the key German radar station on the island of Scarpanto, between Crete and Rhodes. Between our base in Turkey and Scarpanto is Alimnia. The only way we could reach Scarpanto and back was to stage in Alimnia. The reliable LS 24 and a group of ten SBS were available. As this was an important operation, I picked out Sergeant Miller, Privates Evans, Digger Rice and Gunner Ray Jones, all SBS stars, with Captain Bill Blyth in command. At 2 pm on 5 April I had an Orders Meeting in the well of LS 24. We covered the detail. Sail 4 pm 5 April. Check with MO4 agent latest intelligence about Alimnia. I said to myself, 'These men are so experienced there will be no problem with the operation.' Sub-Lieutenant Tuckey arrived fresh from Beirut and, despite a heavy cold, volunteered immediately.

I was surprised when LS 24 missed its planned radio schedule at 9 am on 6 April. There was no news at all during the day and I began to wonder whether there was something seriously wrong with the Patrol. Luckily we had a bright Greek Army Captain as GSF Liaison Officer. I sent him to Alimnia on the night of 7/8 April to find out what happened and return next day. He reported that there had been a gun battle in Alimnia Harbour and the whole raiding group had been captured. I discussed this with Milner Barry, Lassen and the GSF LO and we agreed that there must have been a tip-off. Shortly afterwards 'S' Detachment handed over to 'M' Detachment and I left the Aegean.

After the war I met Bill Blyth each year at the Ascot Royal Meeting. He told me he had spent the rest of the war as a POW in Germany and I assumed the rest of the Alimnia Patrol had fared likewise. The fact that all the others in the Alimnia Patrol had been executed became known in a strange way. Some years ago it was felt that UN Secretary-General Waldheim was not as impartial as he should have been in dealing with the Russians and there was an investigation into his background. The Wiesenthal Organization in Vienna had some files on Waldheim, which showed that he had served as a Captain in German Army Intelligence in the Balkans during the war. He was in Greece in April, 1944, and had signed a letter mentioning the members of the Alimnia Patrol by name, 'For special treatment under the terms of Hitler's Commando Order.'

It was at that point that the SAS Regimental Association was able to get into the act. We now know how unlucky the Alimnia Patrol were. They were on their way to Turkey hidden in the hold of a stolen fishing boat. They were intercepted in daylight by a motor boat manned by the Brandenberg Group, the Germans' SAS. In the SAS our dead and their families are more important to us than the survivors. The dead have made the supreme sacrifice. Survivors live on. The Alimnia Patrol Memorial Service took place at St Paul's Anglican Church, Athens, in the evening of Wednesday 22 May, 1991. Attending were the relatives of Lieutenant Tuckey, Gunner Jones and Private Evans, together with a large congregation, including the Greek Minister of Defence, the Chief of the Hellenic National Defence General Staff and Her Majesty's Ambassador, Athens.

The service was conducted by the Rev B. Chivers. The first lesson was read by Lord Jellicoe and the second by Jason Mavrikis. I had the honour of unveiling the Memorial Plaque and making the following address:

'By early 1944, Greek and British Raiding Forces were active in the Aegean. These units were the Greek Sacred Regiment, Heros Lokos, and the SBS. They numbered no more than 700 Greeks and 300 British, plus naval and air support, yet they tied down two German Army Groups for the rest of the war. The Raiding Force attacks were carefully co-ordinated by GHQ ME in Cairo.

'Our targets were German garrisons on the Aegean islands, their communications and shipping. The enemy were well armed and equipped and fought hard. It was on one of these operations that the Alimnia Patrol and Levant Schooner 24 were lost.

'Of all the men I knew well and had the honour to command during the last war, the finest were the Alimnia Patrol. In the Special Forces business they were the stars. They had long and successful experience of Aegean operations. Three were decorated for bravery. They were very intelligent, loyal to their comrades and to the SBS, modest and fun to be with.

'Their courage and endurance under interrogation was incredible. They came through their appalling ordeal in triumph. They gave nothing away. To me, one word encapsulates the qualities and spirit of the Alimnia Patrol – it is "excellence".

'Indeed, they were the best of Greece and Britain and they died in order that Greece could be free. I am proud to have served with them.

'Unquestionably, their spirit lives on to this day in the Special Forces of Greece and in the exploits of the Special Air Service Regiment in the Falklands and in the Gulf.'

The inscription on the Memorial Plaque reads:

IN MEMORY OF THE ALIMNIA PATROL
CAPTURED 7TH APRIL 1944
AND LATER EXECUTED

TEL R.E. CARPENTER	RN	L/SGT G.W.J. MILLER MM	SBS
PTE. A.G. EVANS MM	SBS	PTE L.G. RICE	SBS
GNR. R.W. JONES MM	SBS	SEAMAN D. TRIANDADYLLOU	RHN
COXSWAIN M.N. LISGARIS	RHN	SUB/LT A.L. TUCKEY	RNVR
	SEAMAN N. A. VELISSARIOU RHN		

MAY THESE COURAGEOUS MEN WHO DIED FOR FREEDOM
REST IN PEACE

The names of the four SBS are in the Book of Remembrance of the Memorial at the War Cemetery near Athens.

Sub-Lieutenant Tuckey's name is on the Royal Naval Memorial at Portsmouth.

14

With the SBS in the Adriatic

1944–45

In July, 1944, it was decided by Cairo HQ that there was no longer a need for the SBS to be deployed in the Aegean. Their role was better filled by the Greek Sacred Squadron. There was, however, a request for SBS Squadrons to be based in Italy for operations in Yugoslavia and the Adriatic islands. This, sadly, brought my romance with the attractive Thessy Whitfield to an abrupt end and I have often wondered what happened to her since. We flew in DC3s (Dakotas) from Cairo to Bari on 11 August with the heavy stores and equipment following by sea. On arrival in Italy we became part of Land Forces Adriatic (LFA) based at Bari. LFA was commanded by Air Marshal William Elliott and comprised army Commandos, 25-pounder artillery and support elements, LRDG, air and naval forces in support and SBS. Twice a week there was a full operational briefing in the LFA ops room, with all LFA representatives present. Fascinating stuff.

The month was spent in the dreary routine of establishing a main base and moving into it. Monte St Angelo provided a school which could be turned into a main billet, and the surrounding hills and forests of the Gargano peninsula a pleasant and useful training area. The LRDG were already there, so many old friendships were renewed and much good advice received, for LRDG patrols had been operating for some time in Yugoslavia, where they had made close acquaintance with the bravery and comradeship of the ordinary Partisan soldier, and also the obliquity and obstruction of some of their political commissars.

Our main base was set up in a tented camp in an olive grove near the village of Monopoli, on the coast south of Bari.

I wanted to keep in touch with Fitzroy Maclean, who had left the SBS a year before to become Churchill's political and military adviser on Yugoslavia. I flew to the island of Vis which was then the headquarters of General Tito, the commander of the Communist Partisans. Fitzroy was there, wearing a Cameron Highlanders regimental tartan kilt, sitting comfortably beneath an old olive tree writing. He handed me a summary of the complex political and military situation of that day reduced to a single page. It was a brilliant piece of work but Fitzroy always was a born writer with total recall of events. We discussed a number of operations SBS was planning as part of the LFA activity and agreed to keep each other informed.

On 27 August, Lassen, with a newcomer, Lieutenant J. C. Henshaw, was landed with two patrols just north of the Yugoslav-Albanian border with instructions to interfere with enemy communications in the area and, as the main aim, to destroy a railway bridge. The salient points of Lassen's report are worth quoting:

3. NARRATIVE
Landed on night 27/28 Aug 44 at MR 513456 S.W. of GRUDA where LRDG patrol reception party laid on. The party, all total 41 men, proceeded by night, laying up in daylight, to Target Railway Bridge at MR 619422 which was completely destroyed at 2300 30/31 Aug 44. Arrived next morning at Partisan H.Q. in high mountains at MR 595480 which was considered absolutely safe. On morning of 2 Sept 44, this H.Q. was surrounded by 400 USTACHI and GERMANS, and

fighting began. Lt. Henshaw with five men defended one ridge. Later a withdrawal was ordered and carried out successfully except for 1 RE who was taken prisoner together with 2 LRDG personnel after a 3 hr fight.

SBS patrols and 2 remaining LRDG personnel successfully evacuated on night 5/6 Sept 44.

4. INTELLIGENCE
Partisans are very brave and efficient raiders in this area. Number 40 altogether, and do much small-scale raiding on roads and rails. Nearly all enemy troops are USTACHI who are highly trained and skilled in anti-Partisan and anti-SBS work. They are very good.

That the Ustachi should win praise from Lassen is hardly surprising for they were recruited from among the Croat peoples, who throughout history have gained a reputation for producing superb soldiers. Even they must have been astonished by the performance of Lassen and the men he led. One of the instructors at Achnacarry had previously remarked upon Lassen's extraordinarily fast reaction time and his almost miraculous ability to move swiftly 'as if without touching the ground', and on this occasion, according to Henshaw, he seemed to be everywhere at once, and always where danger threatened most. He was invariably followed closely by Shaun O'Reilly and others of his own patrol, and between them they so shocked the attackers with their onslaught that in the evening these withdrew, leaving a gap through which Lassen took his men back to the coastline, where in due course they were met by the Navy and evacuated.

I later ordered Lassen to submit a fuller report, especially with regard to the destruction of the railway bridge. 'Ve landed. Ve reached the bridge. Ve destroyed it,' Lassen grumbled. 'Vat else is there to say?' – exhibiting a disdain for paperwork which will excite the sympathy of a large number of soldiers, but also exhibiting a growing acerbity, as battle fatigue began to erode even his placidity and charm.

Other 'S' Detachment patrols were dropped into the area or sent in by sea, but found themselves up against two new and disconcerting factors. Firstly, they were operating on a continent instead of an island, so there was no surrounding sea across which help or re-supply could come from any angle; secondly, they were no longer operating in a friendly environment where the natives not only greeted and helped them with enthusiasm, but also could be depended upon to maintain at least a 95% screen of security.

These beneficial factors no longer obtained, for if the Partisan leaders were not actually prepared to betray Allied plans to the Germans if they did not forward their own immediate political ends, they were certainly prepared to use every obstructive ploy they could concoct to prevent operations which might adversely affect their own local prestige. As a result, and to the perplexity of many SBS men who thought that the only possible attitude towards the Germans would be of unmixed hostility, they found on occasion that the local guerrilla bands were so bleakly uncooperative that there was no practical alternative but to abort the whole mission, return home and start off again entirely on their own.

The SBS officer who most thoroughly appreciated the new conditions was Lieutenant Ambrose McGonigal, who landed in southern Yugoslavia at the end of August and made not the slightest attempt to inform the local Partisans of his plans. As a result they had to tag along behind in order to discover his intentions. After a long night march, they watched him blow in a railway tunnel and thoroughly wreck nearby installations, having first dispersed the Chetnik guard with Bren-gun fire. He then moved with his party further inland and spent the next two weeks ambushing German patrols, and when more and larger patrols were sent out to investigate the disturbances, ambushing them too. His sense of timing would seem to have been impeccable, for when eventually he withdrew, leaving behind several exasperated Partisan commissars, he and his men had killed or wounded well over fifty German soldiers and an unknown number of Chetniks, derailed a train and thoroughly disorganized the local German command, all in addition to the original tunnel destroyed, for the loss of only one man, killed in the last engagement.

Nonetheless, the atmosphere in which the 'S' Detachment patrols had had to live and operate was vastly different from that to which they had been used. Many of them longed for the sound of Greek voices again, and for the feeling of trust and co-operation they had left behind them in the Greek islands.

We were stepping straight into a full-blown Balkan civil war, with Royalists and Communists fighting each other to the death in Albania and Yugoslavia and I thought I should take the opportunity of seeing for myself what was going on on the ground.

As it happened, in early October there was an 'S' Detachment Patrol operating against the withdrawing Germans in Southern Albania. I decided to join them. The task of delivering officers, men and supplies into the Balkans by parachute at that time fell to SOE – Force 144. A special secure airfield south of Bari was used for this purpose. As all parachute operations took place at night, SOE laid on a special champagne dinner beforehand. The dinner table set for two was candle-lit with banks of flowers around. As I entered the room a dark, wiry Captain with a familiar weatherbeaten face rose to greet me. It was George Tsoucas, and we fell on each other's shoulders. He had had a series of incredible adventures since I last saw him in Rhodes almost two years before. And now he was about to drop into Northern Greece as a British Liaison Officer (BLO). Meeting this charming man again did me a lot of good. I thought to myself as I was driven to the aircraft, that this meeting was a good omen for the operation.

Sitting near the exit door with my parachute strapped on, I did not twig until the DC3 had taken off that I was the only passenger. I took the opportunity of a deep post-prandial snooze. The pilot and crew were American, very experienced in finding the right Balkan valley for worried parachutists. My deep sleep ended when an American hand grabbed my shoulder and a voice yelled over the plane's engine noise, 'Too much cloud, we can't drop you tonight. We'll try again tomorrow.' And they did.

I had one of the best jumps ever – not a breath of wind and so accurate that I had to avoid landing in one of the recognition fires. Some familiar faces appeared out of the darkness to greet me: Stud Stellin, the New Zealand Patrol Commander, Douglas Pomford, Staff Sergeant Jenkins – the Soldiers' Friend, and others. I had landed in a small valley with wooded sides. It was half moon. I saw some animals moving about in the trees, which I took to be mules. They approached as the fires were put out and, when the three standard and one red parachute containers were loaded on, we then moved off. In the red container were a large bag of gold sovereigns and personal mail; the others had ammunition, rations, medicines and personal equipment.

My feelings were a mixture of relief that my first operational jump was painless and interest as to what the Albanians and their wild country were like. As we were moving as a heavily laden group up a steep track out of the valley towards a wooded skyline, a voice behind me in good English said, 'I am Ahmed, your interpreter.' I turned round in the darkness to see a middle-aged man with sharp features wearing a heavy brown overcoat and a Fedora! We shook hands. He continued, 'I was a cab driver in New York for many years. You will find me very useful in my country, Albania.' And so we did. Our DZ was in a valley with a stream, about 15 kilometres south of the town of Permet. Our task was to operate against the German military withdrawing north from Greece along the road to Permet. We spent the night in some stone farm buildings nearby. I was exhausted.

Next morning, sitting comfortably in an armchair in the farmhouse, I looked out towards the Permet road. With my binoculars I could see the unmetalled road about 3 kilometres away. We were on a small ridge and between us and the road lay a jumble of hillocks and bushes, which I thought could provide concealment and surprise for our attacks. When talking to Ahmed about German movement on the road, he said, 'This had decreased recently. They move by night and lie up in woods by day in order to avoid attack from the air.' I felt it would help our chance of success and reduce casualties if we spent the next couple of days and nights closely inspecting the ground near the road before making a plan to attack. Douglas Pomford had a bad cold and it fitted in that we should stay put for a couple of days so he could recover.

Also, this was a good time for me to get to know James Lees, who had just joined us. We had been contemporaries at Eton. To be fighting the Germans on mainland Europe at last gave us both a feeling of satisfaction. The countryside, with every level space cultivated by primitive ox-drawn ploughs, had an air of timelessness about it. The endless strands of hardwoods – oak, beech, ash and sycamore – were spectacular in the autumn October sunlight.

I was in our farmhouse base admiring the view when Ahmed appeared. He looked grim. Behind him striding up the hill as if they owned it, were three men in ill-fitting khaki battledress, armed to the teeth: belts of '300 ammunition round the shoulders, red star in their caps and fury in their deeply lined faces. As we rose curiously to our feet, the leader stopped, intoning, 'Death to fascism, long live the people,' raising his right fist in a salute. As we fell about laughing, these three stony-faced Communist guerrillas sat down opposite us, glaring. I asked Ahmed, who looked pretty shaken, what was going on. 'These men,' he explained, 'have been sent by the Partisan military leader who commands this area and is responsible for attacks on the Germans using the Permet road. He does not like your arrival on the scene as this will spoil his personal standing with his political and military superiors who are important to him. He suggests that you should move out of the area, as German movement on the Permet road is decreasing anyway, and go north of Permet to the Pogradetz area where the Germans are still withdrawing.' I asked Ahmed to tell the Partisan leader that we would sleep on his idea and let him know the next day. We discussed the idea among ourselves and with Ahmed present. I felt we should move north and get out of the Partisan leader's way. As they said, the German movement on the Permet road was decreasing anyway, while on the Pogradetz road it was not, and I did not want to spoil Admed's rapport with the Partisans. He was going to be around long after we had left Albania, and the Partisans might give us away.

We crossed the Permet road around midnight – no sign of any enemy movement. There were twelve of us in the group including Ahmed, and each of us had a mule and each mule a muleteer. The mules, of which we eventually ended up with twenty-four, carried our Bergens, blankets, ammunition, tinned rations, water, radio and batteries, petrol, battery charger, cooking pots, etc., plus the muleteers' kit. We wore khaki shorts, shirts and badges of rank, with warm pullovers in reverse. The only items we carried ourselves were personal weapons. We pressed on through a Moslem country. Each village had its working mosque and attendant minaret. The crisp autumn air was full of the sound of the call of the faithful to prayer at dawn and dusk. All men wore a white cap and baggy trousers, the women total black. The legacy of centuries of Turkish occupation was very strong.

We were given quite a lot of maize bread baked into heavy round loaves by old crones in the hills. They were utterly inedible. On one such occasion in a village with a pretty fountain I turned to Jenkins, who was also in trouble with the maize loaf. 'Look, after this my diet needs a sea change.' He looked at me painfully and replied, 'Don't worry, sir, leave it to me.' A couple of days later we stopped in the hills and a delicious chocolate soufflé awaited us. This was made from grinding down the contents of some emergency rations. The Soldiers' Friend looked ecstatic. I said, 'Who did you find?' From the back of the crowd was pushed forward a tiny bald man with thick-lensed glasses, long arms and a pronounced stoop. 'I am Mehmet, King Zog's third sauce chef,' he said. Everyone clapped! I said to myself, 'We need to worry about "our table" no more.'

And so it was. We had a series of spectacular meals of veal and poussin, with rare Albanian steaks soaked in wine, with fantastic sauces. The Soldiers' friend kept asking me for more gold sovereigns from the bag I had with me. I asked, 'Where is all this money going?' 'To pay Mehmet, of course,' came the reply. 'He relies on the Permet black market.' Sadly, we had to pay off Mehmet eventually. He had raised our morale and it was fun while it lasted. Of all the wartime behind-the-enemy-lines operations in which I participated, Albania was the only one with good food!

It was not long before word came that the Germans had left Permet and headed north. Permet was a mixture of charming, old-fashioned Turkish houses and hideous new ones. There was a small, active brewery and airfield. Our task was to find out if the Germans were still using the road from Greece through Pogradetz in Central Albania, and, if so, attack them. The local information from Ahmed was that the Germans had left Central Albania for good. I thought I'd better check this myself. There was on one of the mules a Wellbike, a small motor-bike, and a can of petrol. The distance from Permet to Pogradetz was about 80 kilometres.

I decided to save time by taking four men and two mules for two days' march north from Permet, covering the last bit to Pogradetz back by Wellbike. This worked well. There were no German troops moving; they had recently left. The view of Lake Ochrid from Pogradetz with the Greek and Yugoslav mountains disappearing into the distance was stunning. I realized why that Victorian master landscape artist Edward Lear had fallen for this spot.

Just outside and to the north of the town of Permet there was a marsh into which some duck were flighting. Never one to miss an opportunity to shoot, I asked James Lees if he would like to join me. Ahmed produced a couple of guns and some ancient Italian cartridges. We had fun. James shot a right and left of difficult mallard as the light failed. I missed everything! James' family lives in Dorset and we chatted about the contrast of shooting in Dorset and Albania. Sadly, he died on his next operation on the island of Lussino in the Adriatic. This was a heavy blow to his family and to us.

As there was no further operational need for us to stay in Albania, it seemed to us the most painless way of returning to our base in Italy was to get a Dakota into Permet airfield and fly back from there. This idea was quickly confirmed by a couple of radio messages. I was told by the local Partisan commander, one of the most unpleasant men I have ever met, that the airfield was mined and we were forbidden to use it. A thorough search revealed no mines there. Next day a Dakota with a jolly American crew landed at Permet to fly us back to Italy. The problem was what to do with the twenty-four mules we no longer needed, which were patiently standing around looking unloved! A hilarious scene then developed. The evil-looking Partisan commander: 'These mules are Albanian mules and they are not leaving the country.' Myself: 'They may have been born in Albania, but I have bought them with gold sovereigns. They are King George the Sixth's mules. We are taking them to Italy.'

At this point I turned to the bemused Soldiers' Friend,

'Jenkins, take two men with you and walk the mules to the coast. Let me know when you get there and a landing-craft will pick you up.' I gave him the rest of the gold sovereigns to cover expenses and well remember to this day his cracking salute and 'Sir' as he turned on his heel and left. The mules got safely back to Italy and, after feeding up a bit, did good service in support of Eighth Army in the Italian mountains. This exploit earned the Soldiers' Friend his SAS operational wings for exceptional service.

Not long after returning from Albania I was talking to George Jellicoe outside the SBS office in LFA. Out of the blue he turned to me and said, 'I am going to study at the Army Staff College in Haifa in January next year, and I would like you to take over command of the SBS.' I was flabbergasted. It had never occurred to me in a thousand years that I would command the SBS. I consulted the wise Walter Milner Barry, who was commanding HQ Squadron who urged me to take the job. And so it was that at the ripe old age of 24 I became a Lieutenant-Colonel and the proud commander of an exceptional unit.

To celebrate I decided to fly to Heraklion in Crete to spend Christmas with Anders Lassen, now a Major, who had succeeded me in command of 'S' Squadron. A lot of 'goodies', beer, whisky and cigarettes ensured I had a warm reception at Heraklion airport from Anders and many of the old faithful. As we got into jeeps and headed for the town, Anders leant over and said to me, 'The Germans are bottled up in the north-west corner of Crete. I think we should go there and check that there is nothing we can do against them before we start celebrating Christmas.' I readily agreed and we headed west through Rethymo into the late afternoon sun with the snow-covered White Mountains massively dominating the scene. About 25 kilometres from Canea where the road narrowed between the foothills and the sea, there was a pile of rocks and bits of an old cart blocking the road. As we got out, a couple of armed Cretans appeared. They said that between where we were now and the town of Canea there were strong German defences, some of which I spotted with my binoculars. Apparently, twice a week a fast German MTB dashed by night between Canea and Mytilene to gather supplies. Anders and I felt that the Germans were 'best left alone'.

He and his men had taken over the largest and best hotel in Heraklion for Christmas. Immediately he sent for the town band with all its brass instruments. There were so many tubas, cornets, saxophones and trumpets that they occupied three floors of the hotel and began playing at random. The noise was deafening. The whisky, beer and cigarettes went round. Anders rose, swaying a bit, and ordered, 'You will now play the Danish National Anthem.' No one knew it. He hummed merrily, puffing on a cigarette. The band reciprocated and the whole hotel and street outside shook. The noise, which went on for twenty minutes, was ear-shattering. Everyone in the town came into the hotel. Anders, standing on the stairs, cigarette in mouth, conducted with a napkin. Then the band changed to the Greek National Anthem, and later to 'God Save the King'. And all the time Anders' terrible dog Pipo was peeing on everyone's trousers, mine included. What a night!

In Yugoslavia, during the opening weeks of 1945, SBS patrols found their activities so limited that they were virtually penned into the harbour area of the port of Zara, not by German or even Italian forces, but by the orders of the local Yugoslav leader. The latter made it quite clear that none but his own forces and administrators might take credit for the supplies of food and clothing that were now pouring into the port – from the western capitalist countries, be it said – for the relief of the local population. Neither did he wish it to be believed that any but his own battalions had contributed to the expulsion of the Fascist forces from the region, despite the fact that many locals had actually witnessed men wearing British uniforms in action against the enemy. Those who persisted in such testimony found themselves despatched inland, many never to return.

Against this sad and sordid background, the SBS men waited in grim and cynical mood for further employment and were relieved when orders came for them to expedite the German evacuation of those jagged splinters of land off the Croation coastlines which rejoiced in such names as Krk, Rab and Pag, Lussin and Olib. Though the islands themselves were different in almost every way from those in the Aegean which had recently formed the SBS hunting-ground, the garrisons often consisted of the same men, or at least those who had managed escape or evacuation. They were thus experienced and well aware of both the strengths and the weaknesses of the raiding forces now about to attack them, and their defences were well conceived and soundly constructed.

Surprise, the raider's most important advantage, was therefore almost impossible to achieve, and the recent pattern of large-scale deployment of SBS men against strongly defended positions in what almost amounted to frontal attacks had to be repeated. These attacks, though they would seem to have triggered a spate of desertions by yet more disillusioned Italian troops, were rarely successes in SBS terms.

On the island of Lussin, for instance, the Villa Punta, main billet for the German garrison, was cleared and wrecked and an unknown number of the inhabitants incapacitated to some degree, but the operation cost the lives of Jimmy Lees and Marine Kitchingman, both valued members of 'S' Squadron, and Lieutenant Jones-Parry was badly wounded, as were seven others. Moreover, an attempt to destroy the bridge linking Lussin with the neighbouring island of Cherso had to be abandoned, for the defenders were ready and waiting and determined to remain where they were, underlining a basic principle for raiding troops – that they should not be employed against specific, static or prepared targets.

This was an aspect of which I had always been extremely

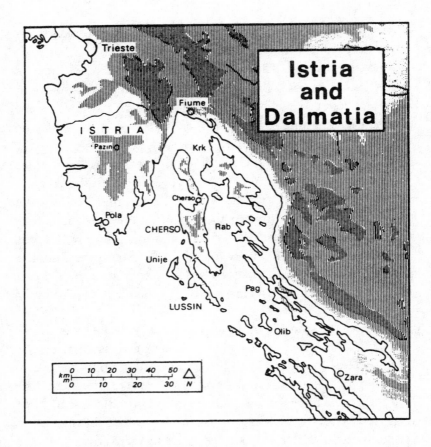

Istria and Dalmatia

conscious. With the prospect of operations on the Adriatic islands yielding ever-decreasing returns and, encouraged by the recent spectacular advance of 'L' Squadron in Greece, I decided to take a squadron, to Istria and perhaps score the same success in Fiume, Pola and Trieste as Patterson had gained in Athens.

In the event I was defeated by the same political machinations. The Yugoslav 45th Partisan Division had occupied the central areas of Istria for some time, extracting food and supplies from the local populace by force or threat. They had been left alone by the Germans in the area since they constituted no immediate menace and were as uninterested in genuinely liberating the area from the Axis forces as had been their opposite numbers in Salonika. The Partisans here had, in fact, no interest in any objective other than occupation first of the eastern half of the peninsula as the Germans withdrew, and then, most important of all, seizure of the port of Trieste, perhaps even at the cost of some casualties, before the British or Americans could get there from northern Italy to organize free elections.

In the meantime, however, the Partisans wished to continue living off the land, consoling the natives for their sacrifices with the thought that they were at least feeding their liberators. Now, suddenly, other liberators were arriving on the scene, liberators who wished and actually intended to attack the Axis forces and thus give a more convincing picture of a liberating force, and who had brought with them not only their own food and stores but also some extra for the indigenous population.

Unfortunately, in Istria the Partisan leaders held the trump cards, for there is little that one squadron of lightly armed raiding troops can do against the wishes of men who have an entire division at their disposal, even one armed and equipped more for policing civilians than fighting against enemy troops, especially when the motives of those leaders are not appreciated at first even in the field, let alone back at headquarters.

So we withdrew back to Italy without having fired a shot against the Germans. It was at the end of this operation that Signaller Wilkinson, came up to me with an ashen face and said, 'You are not going to like this,' handing me a message: 'Anders Lassen died in action in circumstances of great heroism'. This dreadful news was like a knife-thrust deep into one's stomach. We were all silent. How could this happen to the indestructible Anders of all people, who had been through so much enemy action without a scratch? The sooner I got back to base the happier I would feel.

The background to this disaster was that the Eighth Army had spent the winter of 1945 in conditions of excruciating discomfort in the Lower Romagna, a dull, flat, waterlogged breeding-ground for mosquitoes which reaches up from Rimini in the coastal curve to Venice, and inland to Ferrara and Padua. Its lowest and most dismal area constitutes Lake Comacchio, not so much a lake as a flooded area caused by a sand-ridge along the coastline holding back the collected surface water of an area the size of Northern Ireland.

Five miles across at its waist and nearly twenty miles long, Comacchio in the spring of 1945 blocked the northward progress of 'V' Corps on the eastern flank of the Eighth Army. The lake's northern and western shores were held by German troops, and the sand-ridge to the east was blocked by defences manned by soldiers of a Turkoman division, who might have been uncertain as to where their loyalties lay but who could be depended upon to fight like furies once battle was joined. Their defences along the spit of sand were well sited and surrounded with mines, and 'V' Corps patrols had quickly discovered that the Turkomans remained awake and alert during even the coldest nights.

Two marines and two army commandos held the 'V' Corps coastal positions briefed for an assault to bypass the defences on the sand-ridge by pincer movements, one along the line of the eastern shore and the other across Comacchio. The problem for the latter exercise, however, was that it called for the use of deep-water channels, and no one knew where these might run, firstly because pre-war authorities had never felt it worthwhile to chart the lake, and secondly because, even if they had, the channels changed course with every season. All that was known was that for large areas of the lake only six inches of water covered the soft, stinking mud at the bottom, that the water was deeper out in the middle around the few tiny shrub-covered islands which, it was strongly suspected, were used by the enemy as observation points, and that twenty-four inches was probably the average depth.

Twenty-four inches is also the draft of a Goatley float laden with ten men and their equipment, and the draft of a

Carley float is very little less; as for powered landing-craft such as Fantails, they were rightly judged to be too noisy for what was likely to prove a lengthy approach to a hostile shore. It was to help with this difficult specialized task that Brigadier Ronnie Tod asked for Lassen and 2 Patrol SBS to be under his command.

No approach at all could be made unless and until wide channels at least two feet deep had been found and charted, so during the cold dismal nights of March Lassen and his patrols were out from dusk to just before dawn, paddling their folboats through the rushes close up against the dimly seen islands, prodding the ooze below them with measuring sticks and on rare occasions dropping over the side a lead-weighted line. It was slow, bitterly cold work, but as the nights passed the blank spaces on the wall-maps filled up and, to the relief of Brigadier Tod, it became evident that sufficient wide channels did in fact exist for the men of 2nd and 9th Army Commandos to make the sweep across the south-east corner of the lake and go ashore behind the first belt of defences.

Nevertheless on a night which would be especially chosen for its darkness, the chances of assault craft veering off the channel and getting stuck in mud were obviously high, and the solution would be for the men who had charted the channels to lead the assault along them. On the night of 1/2 April, therefore, the folboats slid into the water and the pairs went out to await the dark bulk of the commando craft closing up behind them, while, incredibly but ingeniously, loudspeakers behind them roared out the strains of Wagner's *Ride of the Valkyrie* and the *Lohengrin Preludes* as they had done day and night for a week, to drown the noises of preparation.

The SBS patrols had a long time to wait. The vehicles bringing the commandos and their assault craft bogged down in the approaches to the shoreline; the heavy boats themselves had to be dragged across 1,500 yards of glutinous, stinking mud before reaching water, and then the men they were supposed to carry had to cast around to find the mouths of the channels in which they and their craft could float. It was nearly 0430 before the whole force, with Lassen and his men guiding them, set out on the dark crossing, and as dawn paled the sky a smokescreen made the SBS task that much more difficult, though it undoubtedly helped the assault.

Both commandos landed successfully and Lassen then led his men away to the north where they had been instructed to create a diversion, which they did by themselves, landing and attacking machine-gun posts set in echelon along the narrow roadway threading the spit. Quite soon Trooper Crouch was killed, Shaun O'Reilly severely wounded and the rest pinned down, except for Andy Lassen himself who, indifferent to the fire pouring down the line of the road, raced to the first pillbox and silenced it with grenades. He then used it as cover to shoot through the slit of the next pillbox which he approached and put completely out of action with more grenades, repeating the process with the third and fourth pillboxes along the road.

By now other men of the patrol had come up behind him and a white cloth hung from the doorway of the fifth pillbox. However, as Lassen approached to take its surrender, he was shot from inside by men who quickly paid the price of their duplicity at the hands of Lassen's men.

Lassen himself was still alive when they had finished and they tried to carry him back. But they soon came under heavy fire and were again pinned down and it was during this time that Lassen died.

When I arrived back from Istria everyone at the SBS base at Monopoli was in a state of shock. Even the most hardened of the SBS originals were in tears. I quickly began to assemble facts about the circumstances concerning Anders' death. I spoke to Shaun O'Reilly, wounded and in hospital, and to Les Stevenson in whose arms Anders died. It was from talking to these two that the idea of recommending Anders for the Victoria Cross originated. I then drove to Rimini to have a chat with Brigadier Tod, the commando Brigade Commander, under whose command Anders fought and died. Ronnie Tod, of the Argyll and Sutherland Highlanders, was one of the great Commando leaders of the last war. He talked glowingly about the SBS contribution to the recent battle and Lassen's bravery. I stressed how strongly all of us in the SBS felt that he should be awarded the VC. A faraway look came over the Brigadier's face, as if he was gazing across the deep waters of Lock Fyne towards the distant town of Inveraray. He replied, 'If Anders had survived, an immediate DSO without question, but this is not a VC situation in my own and my staff's opinion.' I tried to talk him round by covering in great detail what Anders had done. No good, he would not budge. Furious, I stormed out of the Brigadier's caravan without saluting.

Driving back to Monopoli, I thought there must be some reason for the surprising line Brigadier Tod was taking. I sent Stewart McBeth, my second-in-command, to find out at Rimini. He quickly discovered that Corporal Hunter, Royal Marines, was being recommended for the VC and the chances of two VCs being awarded for the same action or battle were nil. By chance, an old Eton friend, Tony Crankshaw, was Military Assistant to General Sir Richard McCreery, then C-in-C 8th Army. As that would be the first place in the chain of command, with a Military Secretary's branch handling Honours and Awards, I telephoned Tony, who knew all about the Lassen action at Comacchio, 'We want to get Lassen the VC. Can you help?' He replied, 'Get the citation to me quickly and I will give it a fair wind with the General.' I wrote the strongest possible citation backed by the necessary two witnesses, O'Reilly and Stevenson, got into a jeep and drove to Klagenfurt in Austria, the Corps HQ, and handed the papers in. Thereafter it went like clockwork. The

VC was presented by King George VI to Anders' parents at Buckingham Palace in December, 1945. Happily Corporal Hunter received the VC as well.

★　　★　　★

In June, 1945, shortly after the end of the war in Europe, David Stirling, who had just been released from Colditz, summoned me by telegram to London. Full of interest and anticipation, I took a plane from Rome to Croydon and thence by taxi to the Stirling family flat in North Audley Street. We greeted each other warmly. David had aged a bit but was still full of life and ideas. He waved me to a sofa; his mother produced a large whisky and soda and disappeared. We covered briefly his just over two years in Colditz. He said with a wry smile, 'If I had been 6 inches shorter I wouldn't have been captured in the desert in the first place. My height always and repeatedly gave me away. In prison there was plenty of time to think about and mentally plan a whole range of future SAS operations to be undertaken when I got out. One of these was to form an SAS regiment to support General Chiang Kai-Shek in operations against the Chinese Communists. I have got the Prime Minister interested in and supporting the idea. Would you be interested in forming a squadron of sixty officers and men from your SBS in Italy? You would be in command, as a major – coming down a rank! The other squadron will be commanded by David Lloyd Owen, LRDG, and Roy Farran, 2 SAS.' To me this was a new, unexpected opportunity to operate in the Far East with the SAS, once again led by the amazing Stirling. After so many SAS operations in the Mediterranean, it would be fascinating to get to know China. I felt flattered that the SBS should be included in his star cast. I said to David, 'This sounds interesting. Let me sleep on the idea and let you know in a few days.' I wanted to discuss the project with my parents, whom I had not seen for four years.

Next day my father gave me lunch at the Oriental Club in

172

Hanover Square. He looked tired and a bit older, which is hardly surprising in view of the London bombing, and since he went to Egham and back each day by train to run the Begg Roberts office, which had been moved there from Leadenhall Street in the City. Nevertheless, his mind was active and he wanted to know details of the SBS operations about which I could not write in the letters I had sent him over the years. The mood in England was one of exhilaration now the war in Europe had been won. There were plenty of houses in the West End of London bombed out, with willow herb growing in the ruins. But the light and people's appearance was dull and washed out compared with the warmth and colour of Italy. Strict rationing of food and clothes made me realize how fortunate I had been to be abroad where none of those boring restrictions applied.

My father, a great supporter of my wartime service in the SAS, thought I should go with Stirling to China. So did my mother, with whom I went to Foxboro' Hall by train. She had a boring but important job in a forces canteen in the London docks. She looked well and composed, probably since she had regular meals. At Foxboro' my grandmother, Norah, had aged out of all recognition. There was good reason. Her son, Arnold Vivian, the apple of her eye, serving with the Grenadier Guards in the Western Desert, had been captured near Tripoli. He was two years older than me. As the train taking him and other POWs to Germany was chugging slowly uphill through the Brenner Pass he and a friend, Lord Brabourne, decided to jump train and escape. This they did and hid in nearby woods, but they were unlucky. The Italians were offering large cash rewards to any locals who found Allied escapees and turned them in. Brabourne and Vivian were tried and executed at Bolzano railway station. I had heard about this tragedy and, on my way to Klagenfurt with Lassen's VC citation in my briefcase, I had stopped at Bolzano and photographed the two graves. I gave one photograph to my grandmother and described the site to her, which cheered her up a bit. Shortly afterwards she died peacefully in hospital. She had done a lot to stabilize and give direction to my childhood and youth.

In June, 1945, I became engaged to Jean Henderson. She came from Horsham in Sussex. We had met in the hectic 1939 London season and she was my partner for the Sandhurst June Ball. Off and on during the war we had exchanged letters. My parents were a bit surprised and felt that they were being overtaken by events by my engagement. I was ecstatic. A couple of days later I had a short chat with David Stirling and told him that I was definitely on for China. He was delighted and told me to go back to Italy, form my squadron and be back by 15 August. It was at this point that my father sent the classic telegram to his old WWI buddy, General Adrian Carton de Wiart, who was Churchill's representative in Chungking: 'Look out for my boy David, appearing soon with David Stirling, SAS, to clobber the dreaded Chinese Communists. – Arthur Sutherland.' I never knew how the General replied! The curious thing is that after the war Joan Sutherland, my father's second wife, began living with the General and eventually married him!

Once back in the SBS base at Monopoli, so many people wanted to 'go with Dinky to the Far East' that I had difficulty in selecting sixty. Many were turned away with glum faces. In my scrap-book of the period, there is a charming personal letter to me from Field Marshal Alexander, the C-in-C, saying, 'The reputation you have made for yourselves in your many successful operations in the Mediterranean, the Aegean Islands and the Adriatic coast will never be surpassed, and I would wish you all good luck and God speed wherever you may go.' Ten years later I would impress on my Sandhurst cadet classes that writing personal letters like this is what leadership was all about.

Before leaving for London a couple of memorable dinners were laid on by Jack Nicholson. The whole Regiment sat at a large table in a huge marquee. I remember Simi Soup, a crab bisque, fish à la Petras, a baked turbot, Lamb Levantine with vegetables including Marrow au Athlit, savory Heraklion, grilled Parmesan cheese on toast, Melba Zara, zabaglione, coffee and a fine selection of the best Adriatic wines. I made a speech covering what we had achieved in the Regiment, praising the much lamented Lassen and looking ahead to our new role in the Far East. Jack Nicholson followed me with a sincere and amusing reply.

As we took off from Bari on the morning of 6 August in a Dakota, full of excitement and anticipation for what lay ahead, the plane was full of happy faces in the rows behind me. We landed at Croydon and as soon as the plane had landed and taxied to a halt a mass of people waving flags and shouting gathered round. The ecstatic chant was, 'The war is over.' The Americans had dropped an atom bomb on Hiroshima. I calculated that this had taken place as we headed north over the Alps. It slowly began to dawn on me how mentally and physically exhausted I was after five years of operations behind enemy lines. Perhaps for me, as for many others, it was just as well the fighting stopped then. We had been incredibly lucky to survive. How much longer could this go on? Sooner or later I would have made a fatal mistake.

It seemed to me the most sensible thing to do was to get married to Jean without further delay. This would provide new purpose and direction for my life. So, on 12 September, 1946, at St Peter's, Eaton Square with Jean looking radiant this happened. It was one of the happiest days of my life. We had the reception at 23 Knightsbridge. Quite a number of my old SBS friends turned up to wish me luck, including Douglas Pomford wearing the ribbon of the Military Medal and Bar. It was a lively occasion. By the end of the year the SBS had been disbanded and ceased to exist.

All regular officers at the time at the end of the war had to come down in rank. I joined 1st Battalion Black Watch in BAOR in Duisberg as a major. This was a bit of a culture shock. Luckily, I found myself with some of the Black Watch stars, John Hopwood, Bill Bradford, David Rose and others, who taught me what regimental soldiering is all about. It was fun, and we shot plenty of duck and pheasants. In the desolate ruins of the Ruhr, people searched through the stubble on their knees looking for grains of corn to eat, and the only currency was cigarettes. As soon as wives were allowed out to BAOR, Jean appeared. She was a great asset socially.

In due course we had three children, Sarah, Michael and Fiona, who have all done well in the world.

15

With Greek Raiding Forces in the Civil War

1948

In 1947 I sat the long and testing Staff College Entrance Exam. In January, 1948, I had a telephone message to call a Lieutenant Colonel in the Personnel Branch of the War Office at Lansdowne House, Berkeley Square. He was a jolly-looking Gunner. 'Sit down,' he said. 'I have been looking at your Personal File,' which he had in front of him. 'The Civil War in Greece is a real problem for HMG. I note that you spent a lot of time in the war helping to liberate Greece from the Germans. Officers with your experience and knowledge are badly needed in Greece now to help train Greek Army and Special Forces against the Greek Communists. We have a large British Military Mission based in Athens which we think you should join. How does this idea appeal to you?' The unexpected opportunity to return to Greece, a country of which I had become fond during my SBS days, to help in their fight against Communism seemed too good to be true. I replied that I liked the idea but wanted to have a talk with my wife first. Naturally, as expected, Jean was enthusiastic. 'I will fly out to Athens in due course to be with you,' – and she did.

And so began one of the most interesting, rewarding and entertaining interludes of my life. I went by train to Liverpool Docks. There a small passenger ship of some 5,000 tons was waiting. From the passenger list I spotted Desmond

Buchanan, who was wearing incredibly well-cut plus two's and the Brigade of Guards tie. He was on his way to join the Arab Legion in Amman. We stopped at Malta. There a dotty lady balanced her child on the ship's rail and walked away to photograph him. 'Isn't that a bit dangerous?' I ventured. 'Never mind, he's well insured,' she replied sternly.

A couple of days later I disembarked at Piraeus, eager to get to grips with what was happening. Of all the Balkan civil wars between Royalists and Communists which took place during and just after the last war, that in Greece lasted the longest and was by far the most bitter. A glance at a map shows why. Whoever owns Greece controls the whole of the Eastern Mediterranean. The Greek Communist Party (KKE) had been trying to win power ever since it was founded in 1918. The Greeks commonly distinguish 'three rounds' in the Communist struggle for power. They are in fact three climaxes in a continual process. What distinguished the 'three rounds', however, was that they were attempts to seize power by force of arms. The first round was in 1943–44 during the German occupation when the maritime provinces were wholly in a state of civil war. The second round was the attempt to seize control of Athens and the rest of Greece in December, 1944, shortly after the end of the German occupation. The third round was what is generally known as the Civil War, from 1946 to 1949.

The Headquarters of the British Military Mission to Greece (BMMG) was in the drab-looking Tameon Building in the centre of Athens near the Grande Bretagne Hotel. I reported for duty with Brigadier Ronnie Tod. There was an expectant look on our faces as we were ushered into the presence of the Commander BMMG. Behind a huge desk sat Eric Down, a no-nonsense General whose battered face resembled a prize-fighter's. With a large map of Greece behind him, he waved us to comfortable chairs, 'You have arrived in Athens shortly after the battle of Konitsa in north-west Greece, which took place over last Christmas. The KKE policy was to seize and hold an area of 'Free Greece' containing a major town in which a 'provisional democratic government' could be established. Konitsa was chosen for this purpose. It was the town nearest to Albania – 5 kilometres away and an important communications centre.

'The attack, involving ten guerrilla battalions, began on Christmas morning. The Greek Army was taken by surprise. Soon the guerrillas had seized Konitsa town and all overlooking mountain heights except Profit Ilias. A furious battle ensued, lasting four days. The Greek army and government realized the danger to the country if the rebels continued to hold Konitsa. A major counter-attack was launched from the south. The town was re-taken and, during the course of 4 January, the Democratic Army broke off the action and withdrew to Albania. The Battle of Konitsa cost the National Army over 500 casualties. Democratic Army casualties were probably less, but more than 250 were killed. The National Army had suddenly found the will to win and recovered its morale. Symptomatic of the dramatic change was the appearance in Konitsa of Queen Frederika almost before the battle had ended. In Athens the flags were out.'

General Down went on, 'There are still some 26,000 Communist armed guerrillas in the hills, including 3,000 in the Peloponnese and 2,600 in Roumeli. We have a long, hard haul ahead of us. It will take a long time before all these bandits are rounded up, killed or put behind bars.' It took until December, 1949. 'But we believe,' he went on, 'that the fall of Konitsa is the turning-point in this terrible civil war.' He was right. Before we saluted and left, the General turned to me and said, 'There is someone who you know well waiting for you to arrive in Athens – Colonel Kalinski commanding Greek Raiding Forces' (GRF).

I walked quickly to the office address I had been given. I knew the Colonel was there because of the smell of the Balkan cigarettes he smoked. With my mind anchored on the good Aegean days I was ushered in. Looking fit and relaxed,

Colonel Kalinski greeted me warmly, his face breaking into a smile of welcome. Calling in his interpreter, he quickly came to the point. The existing system for selecting and training GRF reinforcements based on its own training centre at Vouliagmeni was inadequate. Recently, some reinforcements had been killed for lack of proper training. Three men went to get water from a spring. They were shot dead by hidden gunmen waiting for them. He turned to me and said, 'David, please take charge of the British training effort at Vouliagmeni and help us to sort this problem out.'

At that time there were two British infantry battalions stationed in Greece, one in Salonika, the other south of Athens on the coast at Aliki. I managed to get myself attached to the DCLI at Aliki, 15 minutes' drive from Vouliameni. I had a jeep and a good driver, Corporal Sharp. At Vouliagmeni there was a British training team of three good men, Sergeant-Major Kelly, Gordons, and Sergeant Holden, Norfolks, and Pickering, RA, we wore the BMMG insignia, the Greek National colours surmounted by a royal crown on the left breast pocket.

I looked at some of the GRF recruits' weapon handling and use of ground, which was full of simple mistakes. Luckily the training base Commander had on his staff an excellent interpreter, Captain Paul Poulios. It seemed to me that two of us should go and join a GRF company in Roumeli with Poulios to find out what the training requirement for reinforcements exactly was.

On the way north we stopped in Lamia for the night. Thanks to massive help from the USA, the road was open and all the main bridges rebuilt. This was the Truman Plan in action. Greece's essential road network was in this way restored and opened up reasonably quickly. The Americans provided weapons, equipment, food and trucks to get Greece going. The US military effort was led by General van Fleet.

The mountains of Roumeli are spectacular for their rugged steepness and honey-coloured dawn sky. Looking at this halycon scene, one forgot that lying low, concealed in the endless woods and steep valleys, were skilled Communist gunmen ready to die rather than surrender. We stopped at the village of Oiti to get information and water. Masses of villagers of all ages crowded round. Everyone took a long rest in the blazing heat. According to the locals the track north was clear. The company moved out of the village at dusk. Two gunmen opened up and disappeared, killing one and wounding another. Sergeant-Major Kelly and Sergeant Holden were on the spot. There was some confusion in the company and no one immediately took charge. There was no prepared drill for what to do next. No operational procedures existed covering day and night movement in Communist-dominated areas which had been rehearsed beforehand on training exercises. The company was making a lot of noise talking among themselves, which could be heard far away. Some rubber-soled boots were needed. More time should be spent on physical fitness and marching under heavy loads in the mountains.

'Could do better' was our – Poulios, Kelly, Holden and Sutherland – considered opinion after two weeks with the company in the field. We had a long, constructive talk at Vouliameni with the base Commander there. He was very sympathetic to our training ideas. I remarked that it was clear from our observations in the field that reinforcement training needed to be tougher and more closely geared to the operational requirements of Raiding Forces. There had to be a new training course modelled on the SAS selection process.

We then drew up a proposed programme for a six-week selection course. This followed the SAS reinforcement training philosophy: only volunteers, physical fitness, mastery of weapons, initiative, determination, independence of mind, self-sufficiency, compatibility, and a three weeks' basic RF training package at Vouliameni. This included day and night PE, how to use ground, SOPs, weapon firing, load marching. This to be followed by three weeks' advanced RF training at the local mountain training area at Parnis, north of Athens, to include SOPs, map reading and navigation, heavy load-carrying, how to receive an air drop of supplies, tactical problems likely to appear on operations. The course was to end with an 80-kilometre exercise and march from Parnis to Vouliameni via Hymettus. Anyone who failed to make the grade on selection would be returned to unit (RTU).

The proposed new selection training was approved by Colonel Kalinski. The first course took place in October, 1948. I found it hard going, particularly the 80-kilometre march. I suggested to Colonel Kalinski that he might like to be at Vouliameni to present Raiding Force badges to men who had successfully completed their training. This he did.

I wanted to stay on in Greece with Raiding Forces during 1949, but had to return to England for a year's study at the Staff College. Meanwhile the Civil War in Greece dragged on for another year.

It is good to know that the Raiding Force of Greece base at Megalo Pefko is named after General Kalinski.

16

MI5

From 1952 to 1955 I worked as an instructor at the Royal Military College, Sandhurst, and had the good fortune to be there when King Hussein of Jordan was a cadet. A year before my job there was due to end, I began thinking about what to do next and drove to Cringletie to consult my father. I felt that, because of the nuclear stalemate, war in Europe was unlikely. I needed to know when I would command the 1st Battalion, the Black Watch, the aim of all ambitious regimental officers. The Colonel of the Black Watch was General Neil McMicking, a contemporary of my father. I drove to see him in his house overlooking the River Tay. He picked out a book from a nearby shelf and opened it. 'You, David, will follow Nigel Noble in 1962.' I was dismayed – fifteen years as a major between commanding the SBS in war and the Black Watch in peace. At that time promotion in Highland Regiments in peacetime was snail-like. I decided to leave the Army in 1955. My father thought there might be an opening for me in MI5 with important work on national security and nice colleagues to work with. He wrote to John Marriott, Head of Personnel in MI5, whose sister had married a close friend in the tea business.

I had several meetings with John Marriott at Leconfield House, Curzon Street, the Security Service Head Office. In due course I signed up for a 25-year career. My wartime experience and background saw to it that I was posted to the counter-sabotage team in 'C' Branch. Joining the Security Service felt like becoming part of an exclusive monastic order like the Jesuits. The DG was Sir Dick White, the outstanding intelligence officer of his generation.

Working in Leconfield House was like joining a beehive; it hummed with activity. There were about 1,000 men and women in the Service. Some of the most beautiful girls imaginable worked in the Registry in the basement. Their job was to carry files about the office. They reported to a supervisor who looked like a prison wardress. When I joined MI5 the security authorities' image was in disarray. The spies Burgess and McLean had fled to Russia in 1951. There was much chat over lunch in the canteen over what to do about Philby, the suspect spy in MI6. He was a born deceiver. He had been interrogated by all the stars, including Bill Skardon and Dick White himself. But Philby was far too bright to be trapped in interrogation. I said, 'Since Philby is a heavy drinker, why don't you put cyanide in his whisky?' Dick White turned on me, blue eyes flashing. 'Sutherland, that is unethical conduct.' That was the end of the conversation. Some years later, Philby confessed to his SIS controller, Nicholas Elliott, in Beirut, and fled to Russia. Of all the five English secret Communists recruited by the Russians when students at Cambridge University in the 1930s, Philby did by far the most damage to British interests.

Keeping the security of UK key points under review fell to the Security Service. I spent a lot of time inspecting and reporting on the security of ports, airports, power stations, etc, against the threat of sabotage.

★　　★　　★

Returning home to Camberley in mid-May, 1955, Jean told me, 'Brian Franks is after you. He wants you to lunch with him at the Hyde Park Hotel.' At that time Brian was

Chairman of the SAS Regimental Association and a star in the hotel business. He had commanded 2 SAS with great distinction in the war. He had married Zoe Quilter, Raymond's sister, so we met often in Suffolk. A table was set for two in a private room where we enjoyed an excellent lunch. Out of the blue Brian asked if I would like to take over command of 21 SAS from Ian Lapraik next year. I said, 'This sounds a splendid idea. Let me check with Jean and let you know.' John Marriott gave me MI5's blessing.

On 10 January, 1956, I travelled by Underground from Green Park to King's Cross to take over command of 21 SAS. The unit occupied one of the great Victorian TA Drill Halls at 17 Duke's Road off the Euston Road. Waiting for me were three men I knew well: John Woodhouse, Second in Command, Ned Pinnock, QM, and Bob Bennett, RSM. I found two operational Squadrons, 'A' and 'B', at Duke's Road and a signal squadron at White City.

1956 was dominated by the Suez Crisis. Our task was to attack Egyptian Air Force planes at Cairo West. We would start from Libya, using Land Rovers, and drive east. Some alert person in the Foreign Office examined the Libyan Treaty and found that it was illegal for Libyan territory to be used to attack Egypt. The SAS task was, therefore, changed to destroy Egyptian Air Force planes at Heliopolis airport. This meant a parachute operation mounted from Cyprus. I remember General Templer, the CIGS, sending for me. I told him I was a bit uneasy about the legal aspect of using civilian TA men in such an exposed operation. He replied, 'Don't worry, we will enlist them as Regular soldiers.' In the event, this operation never took place which in the circumstances, was probably just as well.

1956 was also the year of the Hungarian uprising. I recall David Stirling telephoning me, 'I have been in touch with General Bill Donovan. We need to know more about what is happening in Budapest. Do you have in 21 SAS a small team with radio we can send in and report back?' But, before anything could be done, the Red Army had crushed all resistance.

The two-week TA camp on Salisbury Plain in August of 1956 was a shambles. Camping with us was the Joint Reserve Reconnaissance Unit (JRRU). This unit was geared to providing information deep in the enemy's rear, like the LRDG in the war. I convinced Bob Bennett that, in Special Force history, the LRDG was in action years before David Stirling had thought of the SAS. Soon JRRU became 23 SAS, and a new, realistic SAS operational future had arrived.

Also in 1956 I persuaded the Portsmouth Company of the Hampshire Parachute Battalion TA to join 21 SAS as the 3rd Squadron. This was a great success. They were excellently trained. Also Major Dare Newell, the SAS visionary, moved from the Far East to be G2 in DLAW. In January, 1960, I handed over 21 SAS to the insurance broker, Jim Johnson.

In retrospect it is a miracle the post-war SAS survived, let alone flourished as it does today. Several times it was touch and go. Our salvation depended on a few, very few, dedicated visionaries and persistent champions at the right place at the right time.

★   ★   ★

In July, 1956, Sir Dick White left MI5 to take over MI6. We had a farewell drinks party for him in the roof garden at Leconfield House. He was succeeded as DG by Roger Hollis, whom we all knew as 'Uncle Roger'. It was a bit of luck for me that Uncle Roger appeared on the scene as I soon found out that he wanted to expand Security Service counter-sabotage advice to the newly independent countries in Africa. Between 1957 and 1962 I spent a lot of time in Africa, the Gulf and the Indian sub-continent, giving counter-sabotage advice for key installations. There were helpful SLOs in all these places with high-level contacts. I remember particularly the Kariba hydro-electric project. The plans showed the distribution transformers were sited north of the Zambezi, to reduce the distance of the transmission towers to Kitwe in the Copper Belt. This seemed to me a bit unnecessary, dangerous and it would be far more sensible to site them south of the river, so reducing the chance of terrorist attacks. This is, of course, what happened.

In the Gulf I advised oil companies from Kuwait to Muscat on how they should protect their vital, vast and vulnerable installations against sabotage and later terrorism. This required an annual visit. Before and after each trip I had a long chat with Uncle Roger. Anyone who could believe he was spying for Russia, as was later alleged, needs their head examining.

When I returned from the Gulf in 1961 I found a letter from Dr Gough Stewart, the Hendersons' family doctor, asking me to call on him. To my horror he told me that Jean had a fatal kidney condition and would live about another 18 months. I was stunned, and asked for a second opinion which confirmed our worst fears. Jean's sister had died of kidney failure. Jean was magnificent as we entered a nightmare period, with her gradually becoming weaker. All my family and friends rallied round, but there was nothing they could do. John Marriott and the Service were particularly helpful and supportive. Before tragically dying in March, 1963, Jean made this typically generous remark: 'David, you are 42. You have your life ahead of you. Marry someone nice soon – it will be good for you and the children.'

As it turned out, I did not have long to wait. In August, I was shooting grouse with Alastair Balfour at Dawyck near Peebles. We were starting to leave for the shoot when I noticed a stunning-looking woman being ignored by Malcolm Wolfe Murray, who was fiddling around with his gun, dog and cartridges. I said, 'Come with me, Mrs Hotchkiss. Malcolm likes to miss his birds in solitude!' And so our romance began. Christine is a Polish landowner's daughter, a classic beauty with high cheek-bones, green eyes and hair like burnished gold. We got married in New York the following year, and have been happy ever since. An historian and author, she had written four books about important women in European history, including *The Princess of Siberia*, the Decembrist classic romance.

In the 1960s there were Security Liaison Officers (SLOs) in Washington and every Commonwealth country around the world. They provided a secure, useful, professional link with Security Service Head Office in London and the security authorities in the country concerned. For some time I had had my eye on becoming SLO Pakistan. John Marriott knew this and shortly after our wedding I found myself in a PIA jet heading towards Karachi. Christine followed ten days later. I was met by Norman Himsworth, the SLO. He had good contacts in Karachi, Rawalpindi and Dacca. East Pakistan was part of my bailiwick. He handed over a large list of social contacts, whom Christine and I entertained in a big way.

Sir Maurice James was High Commissioner. He was one of the diplomatic stars of his generation, later becoming Head of the Foreign Service and a Life Peer. We got on well and often the four of us, Maurice and Elizabeth James, Christine and I, walked in the hills above Rawalpindi. As we tackled the next steep track, Sir Maurice would say, 'The partition of India and the partition of Ireland are two of the worst man-made tragedies of our time. Result: India and Pakistan arming to the teeth with nuclear weapons they cannot afford, and the fearsome, uncompromising IRA.'

The creation of Pakistan as a country has not worked for two reasons; involvement of the Pakistan Army in politics, and corruption. Our great legacy to India is that their huge army shuns politics.

Christine ran a marvellous house with delicious food. We entertained a lot of interesting Pakistanis from Government Departments and their wives. We lived well: two cooks, chauffeur, gardener, an imposing office with two secretaries. It was sad to pack up, leave friends and return home.

Roger Hollis was succeeded as DG by Martin Furnival Jones in 1965. There were a number of allegations from Secret Intelligence sources and from James Angleton of the CIA about a ring of five men spying for Russia. Four were already known: McLean, Burgess, Blunt and Philby. Because the Security Service was such an obvious target for the Soviets, it was felt the fifth spy was probably there. This caused a highly damaging mole-hunt in MI5 throughout Furnival Jones's time as DG. I twigged that something odd was happening when, out of the blue, Peter Wright telephoned. He asked me to come and see him in his office. Peter Wright was a highly skilled electronics engineer from Marconi. He was an expert on the use and placing of microphones for Intelligence purposes.

He started by asking how well I knew Roger Hollis? I said, 'Before and after each time I go abroad, we have a 15-minute chat. I think Uncle Roger is strong and effective. Why do you believe he is untrustworthy?'

'I have some information about him which is damaging. I cannot reveal the source.'

And with that finale he showed me the door. Peter Wright conducted the interview like an angry, ambitious fox-terrier worrying at a bone. I still wonder why such a sensitive job had been given to such a confused man? I thought he was mentally unstable. At any rate I never saw Wright again.

The mole-hunt involved Graham Mitchell as well as Roger Hollis. Mitchell was former Head of Intelligence, MI5, and an international chess-player. It was a distressing thing in retirement to know your telephone is being tapped and mail opened. It was the Security Service's post-war nadir.

When Sir Michael Hanley became DG the first thing he did was to stop the mole-hunt. Some years later John Cairncross, formerly of the Treasury and on the fringes of investigation, admitted he was the fifth man.

Michael Hanley had risen to the top of MI5 through 'C', the Protective Security Branch. We got on well and in him we had a DG who really knew what protective security was all about. Between 1972 and 1980 as a senior officer, equivalent to an Army Brigadier, I was able to expand and get some exceptional men into C4, at a time when the threat from the IRA and international terrorism was severe. They included Ken Ritchley, formerly RAF, on aviation security, Hugh Fraser, formerly Colonial Service, on key point protection, John Coghill, formerly Royal Army Ordnance Corps, arranging the bi-annual international conferences, on terrorist devices and methods. Delegates came from all over the world. Sandy Stuart, formerly Scots Guards, excelled in chatting up police on the many counter-terrorist exercises we had. Also, because of my links with the SAS, I helped the Home Office Response Team and police negotiators on many counter-terrorist exercises before and after the Iranian Embassy siege.

★   ★   ★

I would like to end this book with my three contemporary heroes, one Scot, one Greek, one Jordanian. The first two, sadly, are dead; the third, mercifully, still alive. All are fearless, romantic, inspirational leaders. It was my good fortune to meet and serve with them.

★   ★   ★

Word gets round the noisy Kabrit Camp that the Colonel wants to see me. Behind a huge desk is David Stirling, wearing well-cut KD and DSO ribbon. He rises to greet me. With his unusual height, fine features and fascinating ideas about future SAS operations, there is something compelling about him.

He wants to know about Operation ANGLO. 'How many planes have been destroyed?' 'Around a dozen at Calatos and probably more at Maritsa,' I tell him. He smiles. We talk for about 20 minutes. The SBS will be the tool for the forthcoming attacks on 'the soft underbelly of Europe'. Fascinating stuff. At the end he says, 'From now on I would like you to wear SAS operational wings.' For me, aged 22, this is a totally unexpected and incredible honour. That night I get stoned!

★   ★   ★

It is 1943. It is night. I am in a Dakota aircraft heading north towards Samos. Beside me in parachute gear is a thick-set man with a brown, lined face, old enough to be my father. I am delighted he is jumping, not me.

As we approach the dark mass of the island below, he turns to me and says, 'Sutherland, is that enemy fire coming towards us?' I reply, 'No Colonel, those are sparks from the engine. It's old and needs decarbonizing.' With that slender reassurance he jumps into the void and disappears. It is Colonel Tsigantes, the Commander of Greek Raiding Forces, first parachute jump. I return safely to base.

★   ★   ★

I am standing alone in Old College Hall of Study. Outside shafts of sunlight herald a glorious summer day. I have just shaken hands with His Majesty King Hussein of Jordan. He is leaving Sandhurst today.

I say to myself, if this remarkable seventeen-year-old avoids assassination, which sadly his illustrious grandfather did not, he will, in time, become a tremendous force for stability in the turbulent Middle East.

Bibliography

The Black Watch and the King's Enemies
    by Bernard Fergusson – Collins, 1950
A History of the 6th Battalion The Black Watch, 1939–1945
    by Brian Madden – D. Leslie, Perth, 1948
The Commandos
    by Charles Messenger – William Kimber, London, 1985
Combined Operations 1940–1942
    Published by HMSO, 1943
Commando
    by John Durnford Slater – William Kimber, London, 1953
SBS in World War Two
    by C. B. Courtney – Robert Hale, London, 1983
A History of the SAS Regiment
    by John Strawson – Secker and Warburg, London, 1984
Eastern Approaches
    by Fitzroy Maclean – Jonathan Cape Ltd, 1949
Cairo in the War
    by Artemis Cooper – Hamish Hamilton Ltd, 1989
Providence Their Guide – The Long Range Desert Group 1940–45
    by David Lloyd Owen – George Harrap & Co Ltd, 1980
Special Boat Squadron
    by Barrie Pitt – Century Publishing Co Ltd, 1983

The Filibusters
    by John Lodwick – Methuen & Co Ltd, 1947
Crete – The Battle and the Resistance
    by Antony Beevor – John Murray, 1991
The Special Air Service
    by Philip Warner – William Kimber, 1971
Anders Lassen VC MC of the SAS
    by Mike Langley – New English Library, 1988
Report on Operation ANGLO, Rhodes, September, 1942
    by George Vroohos, Attorney-at-Law and Historian,
    living in Rhodes. Published by the Municipality of
    Rhodes, 1988. Copies of Italian Reports signed by the
    Italian Governor of the Italian islands of the Aegean Sea,
    Admiral Inigo Campioni, translated by Sheila Gruson.
*The Aegean Mission – Allied Operations in the Dodecanese
    1943*
    by Jeffrey Holland – Greenwood Press, 1988
The Struggle for Greece, 1941–1949
    by C. M. Woodhouse – Hart Davis MacGibbon Ltd,
    1976
Something Ventured
    by C. M. Woodhouse – Granada Publishing Ltd, 1982
Xenia – A Memoir, Greece 1919–1949
    by Mary Henderson – Weidenfeld and Nicolson, 1988
Eleni
    by Nicholas Cage – Random House, NY, 1983
To War with Whitaker
    by Countess of Ranfurly – William Heinemann Ltd, 1994
The Phantom Major
    by Virginia Cowles – Collins, London, 1958
After the Battle Series: No. 90
'The Battle for Leros'
    Published by Battle of Britain Prints International Ltd.,
    London
Sandhurst
    by Alan Shepherd – Country Life Books, 1980

Hussein of Jordan
    by Gerald Sparrow – George Harrap and Co Ltd, 1960
Hussein of Jordan – a Political Biography
    by James Lunt – MacMillan, London, 1989
Forgotten General – a Life of Andrew Thorne
    by Donald Lindsay – Michael Russell, 1987
Kommando – German Special Forces of World War 2
    by James Lucas – Army and Armour Press, 1985
A Matter of Trust – MI5 1945–72
    by Nigel West – Weidenfeld and Nicolson, 1982
Spycatcher
    by Peter Wright – Viking, 1987
The Perfect English Spy – Sir Dick White and the Secret War 1955–90
    by Tom Bower – Mandarin, 1995

Index

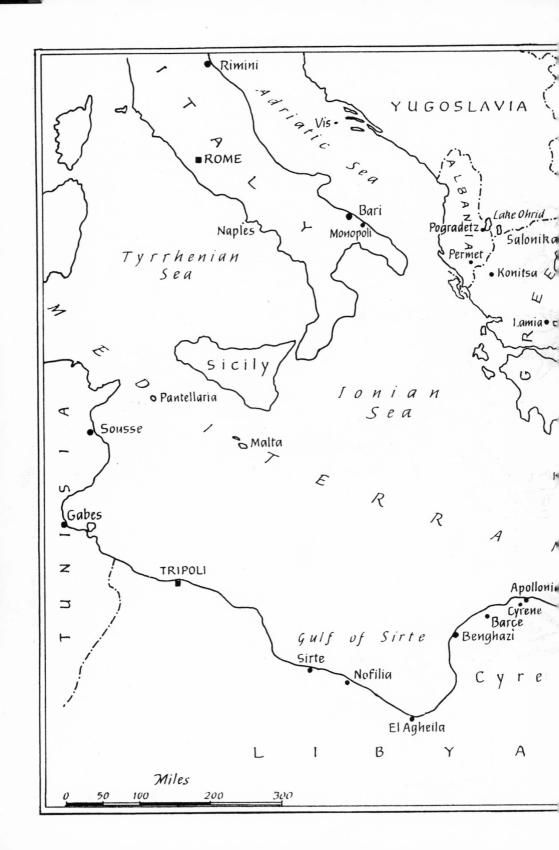

Rimini

Adriatic Sea

YUGOSLAVIA

Vis·

I T A L Y

■ ROME

Bari

Naples

Monopoli

ALBANIA

Pogradetz

Lake Ohrid

Permet

Salonika

Konitsa

Tyrrhenian Sea

Lamia

G R E E

Ionian Sea

S i c i l y

○ Pantellaria

M E D I

Sousse

○ Malta

T E R R A

N

Gabes

TUNISIA

TRIPOLI ■

Apolloni

Cyrene

Barce

Benghazi

Gulf of Sirte

Sirte

Nofilia

C y r e

El Agheila

L   I   B   Y   A

Miles

0   50   100   200   300